LETTERS OF JOHN NEWTON

D1331288

LETTERS OF

JOHN NEWTON

THE BANNER OF TRUTH TRUST
78b Chiltern Street, London, w.1

THE BANNER OF TRUTH TRUST
3 Murrayfield Road, Edinburgh EH12 6EL
P.O. Box 621, Carlisle, Pennsylvania 17013, USA

*

This selection from John Newton's correspondence first published by the
Banner of Truth December 1960

Reprinted 1965
Reprinted 1976
Reprinted 1984
Reprinted 1990

Letters 1–7 and 10–19 are from letters signed *Omicron* (1774)
and *Vigil* (1785); the remainder are from Newton's best-known
work, *Cardiphonia* (1781).

ISBN 0 85151 120 1

*

This book is set in 10-point Bookprint and
printed and bound in Great Britain by
BPCC Hazell Books
Aylesbury, Bucks, England
Member of BPCC Ltd.

CONTENTS

CONTENTS

INTRODUCTION

IN the first half of the 18th century England was in a state of religious and moral decay. For many years the land had been sinking into darkness and paganism. Intemperance and immorality, crime and cruelty were increasingly becoming the characteristics of the age. The National Church was in such a dead condition that instead of being the salt, preserving the nation from corruption, she was only adding to the immorality by weakening the restraints which Christianity imposed on the lusts of men. The teaching from the pulpit consisted of natural theology and cold morality which were utterly impotent to awaken the Church or to stem the flood of iniquity. If the nation was to be saved the Church would first have to be revived. And that is what took place. What the arm of flesh could not do the arm of omnipotence accomplished. God was pleased to send a mighty revival which in the course of fifty years transformed the religious and moral life of the land.

Although this great awakening was entirely the work of the Holy Spirit yet God used human instruments to effect the change. Some of the leaders of the movement are well known to us, such as George Whitefield and John Wesley. They were the early leaders in the awakening and, because of their widespread labours, overshadowed such eminent contemporaries as William Grimshaw, John Berridge, Daniel Rowlands and William Romaine. As the revival movement spread, a second generation of leaders emerged. Chief among them was John Newton, the once infidel mariner and servant of slaves, who became, through the grace of God, a humble Christian and devoted minister of Christ.

The gifts of the Holy Ghost to the Church are various and manifold so that all members have not the same office. This was clearly seen among the leaders of the Evangelical Revival. Each had his own position to fill and each had his special gift from God. Newton's gift was that of dealing with individual souls and he accordingly became the great spiritual director of souls in the Evangelical Movement. Writing to one of his correspondents, he speaks about ministers, according as their gifts differ, being led to consider some particular branch of the system of divine truth, and he goes on to say, " So far as I can judge, anatomy is my favourite branch; I mean the study of the human heart with its workings and counter-workings as it is differently affected in a state of nature or of grace, in the different seasons of prosperity, adversity, conviction, temptation, sickness and the approach of death."

There is no doubt that Newton had been peculiarly prepared for this aspect of the ministry by the course of his early life. Born in London in 1725, deprived of the godly influence of his mother before he was seven years old, he was but two years at school before he went, at the age of eleven, on his first voyage with his father, a sea captain. From that time till the age of thirty, when his health was broken by a stroke, Newton endured the wild rigours of a life before the mast. The vicissitudes of his maritime career are well known. How he was press-ganged aboard a naval vessel; how he was flogged when captured after desertion; how his love for the youthful Mary Catlett preserved him from suicide; how he was released from the navy only to join in the slave traffic across the Atlantic; how he was reduced almost to death on the Guinea coast and delivered by a friend of his father's—these are all things with which the reader of Newton's biography will be familiar. Throughout these sad events there ran a divine purpose; and while Newton forgot the Saviour whom his mother had so often commended to him in childhood, and while he became, like one of old, a " blasphemer and injurious," it was all leading to a day when he was brought to say :

> " Bow'd down beneath a load of sin,
>   By Satan sorely pressed,
>   By wars without, and fears within,
>   I come to Thee for rest."

After Newton ended his seafaring days he became tide-surveyor in Liverpool, a thriving slave port with a population of 22,000. It was here that Newton first heard the great evangelist, George Whitefield, and soon he came to know other leaders of the Evangelical Revival such as William Grimshaw and Henry Venn. His own thoughts were now turned to the ministry, and after several disappointments he was at length settled in 1764 in the Buckinghamshire parish of Olney—a name immortalized by the hymns which he and Cowper wrote for their mid-week meetings. Such facts as these need to be borne in mind by the reader of these letters. The dreadful condition from which he had been saved, the long struggle he went through before he came to a clear understanding of the Gospel and the years of patient waiting for an opening in the Church, all served to prepare Newton for this work. He was given a thorough knowledge of the workings of the human heart and of the Lord's dealings with His people.

In his sixteen years at Olney, Newton found a good field for exercising his gift. The people of that country district were simple folk and ready to speak all their heart. With the publication of his *Authentic Narrative* (in his first year at Olney), giving an account of his early life, conversion and call to the ministry, his fame became more widespread and people came from far and near to seek his counsel and help.[1] His friendly and hospitable home at Olney, and later in London,[2] was a place to which the troubled and tempted resorted. They found in him one who had been a worse sinner than themselves and who could enter into their experiences with tenderness and sympathy.

Those who could not come to see him sought his help by letter and it was this that brought the best out of Newton. Marcus Loane describes him as " the letter writer *par excellence* of the Evangelical Revival " and says that " this was his distinctive contribution to that great movement." He was not unconscious of his gift and of his usefulness in this department

[1] On one occasion he was even visited by an Indian chief who had been converted under Whitefield in North America, and who became a preacher among his own tribe, the Mohicans.

[2] He became minister of St. Mary Woolnoth in 1779, where he continued to preach until almost the end of his life in 1807. Being advised by Richard Cecil in 1806 to discontinue preaching, he gave the memorable reply, " I cannot stop. What, shall the old African blasphemer stop while he can speak?"

and his diligence was prodigious. "It is the Lord's will," he
says, " that I should do most by my letters."

Newton's letters are the expression of his inmost being; he
speaks of his correspondents as those to whom " when I can
get leisure I send my heart by turns." But while they thus
reflect the work of grace in his own life they are at the same
time a mirror of the Evangelical thought and practice of his
day. This is particularly helpful to us, for the spiritual life
of the Church of Christ is not always at the same level of
power and purity, and it is all too easy in such an age as our
own to forget the true nature of vital Evangelical religion. In
this connection there are certain things which the pages of this
book bring forcibly to light and of which we need to be reminded today.

The first is that *true Evangelical religion is intensely personal.* It does not consist in the mere attachment to certain
doctrines and opinions which were held by Christians in past
generations, still less does it consist in belonging to a party.
Rather it is something which must be experienced in one's own
soul. "We may grow wise apace in opinions, by books and
men," writes Newton, " but vital experimental religion can
only be received from the Holy Spirit." Because Newton held
to the system of Biblical doctrine which received its formula-
tion in the writings of John Calvin, some might be ready to
think that it was from the great Reformer that he received his
beliefs. This would be totally to misunderstand the nature of
true Evangelical faith. "I should have much to answer for
had I invented it myself, or taken it upon trust from Calvin,"
writes Newton; " but as I find it in the Scripture I cheerfully
embrace it." He had, like every Christian, a personal experience of the truth of Scripture implanted in his soul by the
Spirit of God. He could speak of the sovereignty of God as one
who had witnessed it in his own experience; he could speak of
the grace of God as one who had tasted that the Lord is
gracious; and he could speak of the power of God as one who
was experiencing it in his own life.

The second truth of which Newton's letters constantly remind us, is that *true Evangelical religion produces intense
exercise of soul.* Where the life of God has been implanted in

the soul of man, a warfare begins between the good and the evil, between the new nature and the old. If there is one thing outstanding in Newton's letters, it is, perhaps, the happy combination between spiritual mourning and spiritual rejoicing. Like the Apostle Paul he could cry with one breath: "O wretched man that I am" and, with the next, "I thank God through Jesus Christ our Lord." Writing to one of his correspondents he exhorts thus: "You say you are more disposed to cry, Miserere! than Hallelujah! Why not both together? When the treble is praise and heart-humiliation for the bass, the melody is pleasant and the harmony is good." The purpose of God in showing believers the evil of their own hearts is to make them prize more highly the grace and all-sufficiency of Jesus. In this way they go through life "sorrowful yet alway rejoicing."

Soul exercise is evidence of a healthy spiritual condition. It is at times when religion has been in a flourishing state that soul exercise has been most prominent in the professing Church of Christ. It is the barometer by which we may read the prevailing condition in the Church, the spiritual pulse of the Church indicating the strength or weakness of vital Evangelical religion. This should give us some light on the state of the Church today. When we consider that soul exercise is a term which has almost passed out of our religious vocabulary and that more attention is paid to the outward actions of the Christian life than to the state of the heart, we cannot but come to the conclusion that vital godliness is at a low ebb.

Newton's letters serve to show us in the third place that *true Evangelical religion is intensely practical.* He opens up the truth to his correspondents, not in order that they may admire his wisdom, but that it may influence their hearts and lives. It is only as the doctrines of God's Word are received and believed by us that we can practise Christianity. Many of the problems and difficulties with which his correspondents confronted him were delicate and complicated and we cannot but be struck with his manner of dealing with them. His replies are characterized by practical down-to-earth instruction and sanctified common sense.

All who love to trace the work of God in the soul of man,

all who are troubled with sin and temptation, all who are seeking guidance in the Christian life, will find a deep mine in the letters of John Newton. There are riches abounding here for the poor of Christ's flock. Written in simple flowing language, the letters are *easy* to read. What Dr. Alexander Whyte said of John Newton's Letters is indeed a fair estimate of their worth—" a volume of the purest apostolical and evangelical truth, written in a strong, clear, level and idiomatic English style."

The Publishers,
July, 1960.

LETTER I

A; or, Grace in the Blade. Mark iv. 28.

Dear Sir,

ACCORDING to your desire, I sit down to give you my general views of a progressive work of grace, in the several stages of a believer's experience; which I shall mark by the different characters A, B, C, answerable to the distinctions our Lord teaches us to observe from the growth of the corn, Mark iv. 28. "First the blade, then the ear, after that the full corn in the ear." The Lord leads all his people effectually and savingly to the knowledge of the same essential truths, but in such a variety of methods, that it will be needful, in this disquisition, to set aside, as much as possible, such things as may be only personal and occasional in the experience of each, and to collect those only which in a greater or less degree are common to them all. I shall not therefore give you a copy of my own experience, or of that of any individual; but shall endeavour, as clearly as I can, to state what the Scripture teaches us concerning the nature and essentials of a work of grace, so far as it will bear a general application to all those who are the subjects of gracious operations.

By nature we are all dead in trespasses and sins, not only strangers to God, but in a state of enmity and opposition to his government and grace. In this respect, whatever difference there may be in the characters of men as members of society, they are all, whether wise or ignorant, whether sober or profane, equally incapable of receiving or approving divine truths, I Cor. ii. 14. On this ground our Lord declares, " No man can come unto me, except the Father who has sent me draws him." Though the term *Father* most frequently expresses a known and important distinction in the adorable Trinity, I apprehend our Lord sometimes uses it to denote God, or the Divine

Nature, in contradistinction from his humanity, as in John xiv. 9. And this I take to be the sense here: "No man can come unto me unless he is taught of God," and wrought upon by a divine power. The immediate exertion of this power, according to the economy of salvation, is rather ascribed to the Holy Spirit than to the Father, John xvi. 8-11. But it is the power of the God and Father of our Lord Jesus Christ; and therefore severally attributed to the Father, Son, and Spirit, John v. 21. and ch. vi. 44-63; 2 Cor. iii. 18; 2 Thess. iii. 5.

By A, I would understand a person who is under the draw-ings of God, which will infallibly lead him to the Lord Jesus Christ for life and salvation. The beginning of this work is instantaneous. It is effected by a certain kind of light com-municated to the soul, to which it was before an utter stranger. The eyes of the understanding are opened and enlightened. The light at first afforded is weak and indistinct, like the morning dawn; but when it is once begun, it will certainly in-crease and spread to the perfect day. We commonly speak as if conviction of sin was the first work of God upon the soul that he is in mercy about to draw unto himself. But I think this is inaccurate. Conviction is only a part, or rather an im-mediate effect of that first work; and there are many convic-tions which do not at all spring from it, and therefore are only occasional and temporary, though for a season they may be very sharp, and put a person upon doing many things. In order to a due conviction of sin, we must previously have some adequate conceptions of the God with whom we have to do. Sin may be feared as dangerous without this; but its nature and demerit can only be understood by being contrasted with the holiness, majesty, goodness, and truth, of the God against whom it is committed. No outward means, no mercies, judge-ments, or ordinances can communicate such a discovery of God, or produce such a conviction of sin, without the concur-rence of this divine light and power to the soul. The natural conscience and passions may be indeed so far wrought upon by outward means, as to stir up some desires and endeavours; but if these are not founded in a spiritual apprehension of the perfections of God, according to the revelation he has made of himself in his word, they will sooner or later come to nothing; and the person affected will either return by degrees to his former ways, 2 Peter ii. 20; or he will sink into a self-righteous form of godliness, destitute of the power, Luke xviii. 11. And therefore, as there are so many things in the dispensation of the Gospel suited to work upon the natural passions of men, the many woeful miscarriages and apostasies amongst professors are more to be lamented than wondered at. For though the seed may seem to spring up, and look green for a season, if there be not depth for it to take root, it will surely wither away. We may be unable to judge with certainty upon the first appearance of a religious profession, whether the work be thus deep and spiritual or not; but "the Lord knows them that are his;" and wherever it is real, it is an infallible token of salvation. Now as God only thus reveals himself by the medium of Scripture truth, the light received this way leads the soul to the Scripture from whence it springs, and all the leading truths of the word of God soon begin to be perceived and assented to. The evil of sin is acknowledged; the evil of the heart is felt. There may be for a while some efforts to obtain the favour of God by prayer, repentance, and reformation; but, for the most part, it is not very long before these things are proved to be vain and ineffectual. The soul, like the woman mentioned Mark v. 26, wearied with vain expedients, finds itself worse and worse, and is gradually brought to see the necessity and sufficiency of the Gospel-salvation. A may soon be a believer thus far: That he believes the word of God, sees and feels things to be as they are there described, hates and avoids sin, because he knows it is displeasing to God, and contrary to his goodness; he receives the record which God has given of his Son; has his heart affected and drawn to Jesus by views of his glory, and of his love to poor sinners; ventures upon his name and promises as his only encouragement to come to a throne of grace; waits diligently in the use of all means appointed for the communion and growth of grace; loves the Lord's people, accounts them the excellent of the earth, and delights in their conversation. He is longing, waiting, and praying, for a share in those blessings which he believes they enjoy, and can be satisfied with nothing less. He is convinced of the power of Jesus to save him; but through remaining ignorance and legality, the remembrance of sin committed, and the sense of present corruption, he often questions his willingness; and, not knowing the aboundings of grace, and the security of the promises, he fears lest the compassionate Saviour should spurn him from his feet.

While he is thus young in the knowledge of the Gospel, burdened with sin, and perhaps beset with Satan's temptations, the Lord, "who gathers the lambs in his arms, and carries them in his bosom," is pleased at times to favour him with cordials, that he may not be swallowed up with over-much sorrow. Perhaps his heart is enlarged in prayer, or under hearing, or some good promise is brought home to his mind, and applied with power and sweetness. He mistakes the nature and design of these comforts, which are not given him to rest in, but to encourage him to press forward. He thinks he is then right because he has them, and fondly hopes to have them always. Then his mountain stands strong. But ere long he feels a change: his comforts are withdrawn; he finds no heart to pray; no attention in hearing; indwelling sin revives with fresh strength, and perhaps Satan returns with redoubled rage. Then he is at his wit's end; thinks his hopes were presumptuous, and his comforts delusions. He wants to feel something that may give him a warrant to trust in the free promises of Christ. His views of the Redeemer's gracefulness are very narrow; he sees not the harmony and glory of the divine attributes in the salvation of a sinner; he sighs for mercy, but fears that justice is against him. However, by these changing dispensations, the Lord is training him up, and bringing him forward. He receives grace from Jesus, whereby he is enabled to fight against sin; his conscience is tender, his troubles are chiefly spiritual troubles; and he thinks, if he could but attain a sure and abiding sense of his acceptance in the Beloved, hardly any outward trial would be capable of giving him much disturbance. Indeed, notwithstanding the weakness of his faith, and the prevalence of a legal spirit, which greatly hurts him, there are some things in his present experience which he may perhaps look back upon with regret hereafter, when his hope and knowledge will be more established; particularly that sensibility and keenness of appetite with which he now attends the ordinances, desiring the sincere milk of the word with earnestness and eagerness, as a babe does the breast. He counts the hours from one opportunity to another; and the attention and desire with which he hears may be read in his countenance. His zeal is likewise lively; and may be, for want of more experience, too importunate and forward. He has a love for souls, and a concern for the glory of God; which, though it may at some times create him trouble, and at others be mixed with some undue motions of self, yet in its principle is highly desirable and commendable; John xviii. 10.

The grace of God influences both the understanding and the affections. Warm affections, without knowledge, can rise no higher than superstition; and that knowledge which does not influence the heart and affections, will only make a hypocrite. The true believer is rewarded in both respects; yet we may observe, that though A is not without knowledge, this state is more usually remarkable for the warmth and liveliness of the affections. On the other hand, as the work advances, though the affections are not left out, yet it seems to be carried on principally in the understanding. The old Christian has more solid, judicious, connected views of the Lord Jesus Christ, and the glories of his person and redeeming love; hence his hope is more established, his dependence more simple, and his peace and strength, *cæteris paribus*, more abiding and uniform, than in the case of a young convert; but the latter has, for the most part, the advantage in point of sensible fervency. A tree is most valuable when laden with ripe fruit, but it has a peculiar beauty when in blossom. It is spring-time with A; he is in bloom, and, by the grace and blessing of the heavenly husbandman, will bear fruit in old age. His faith is weak, but his heart is warm. He will seldom venture to think himself a believer; but he sees and feels, and does those things which no one could, unless the Lord was with him. The very desire and bent of his soul is to God, and to the word of his grace. His knowledge is but small, but it is growing every day. If he is not a *father* or a *young man* in grace, he is a dear *child*. The Lord has visited his heart, delivered him from the love of sin, and fixed his desires supremely upon Jesus Christ. The spirit of bondage is gradually departing from him, and the hour of liberty, which he longs for, is approaching, when, by a further discovery of the glorious Gospel, it shall be given him to know his acceptance, and to rest upon the Lord's finished salvation. We shall then take notice of him by the name of B, in a second letter, if you are not unwilling that I should prosecute the subject.

I am, &c.

LETTER II

B; *or, Grace in the Ear*. Mark iv. 28.

Dear Sir,

THE manner of the Lord's work in the hearts of his people is not easily traced, though the fact is certain, and the evidence demonstrable, from Scripture. In attempting to explain it, we can only speak in general, and are at a loss to form such a description as shall take in the immense variety of cases which occur in the experience of believers. I have already attempted such a general delineation of a young convert, under the character of A, and am now to speak of him by the name of B.

This state I suppose to commence, when the soul, after an interchange of hopes and fears, according to the different frames it passes through, is brought to rest in Jesus, by a spiritual apprehension of his complete suitableness and sufficiency, as the wisdom, righteousness, sanctification, and redemption of all who trust in him, and is enabled by an appropriating faith to say, " He is mine, and I am his." There are various degrees of this persuasion; it is of a growing nature, and is capable of increase so long as we remain in this world. I call it assurance, when it arises from a simple view of the grace and glory of the Saviour, independent of our sensible frames and feelings, so as to enable us to answer all objections from unbelief and Satan, with the apostle's words, " Who is he that condemneth? It is Christ that died, yea rather, that is risen again, who is even at the right hand of God, who also maketh intercession for us." Rom. viii. 34. This, in my judgement, does not belong to the essence of faith, so that B should be deemed more truly a believer than A, but to the establishment of faith. And now faith is stronger, it has more to grapple with. I think the characteristic of the state of A is *desire,* and of B is *conflict.* Not that B's desires have sub-sided, or that A was a stranger to conflict; but as there was a sensible eagerness and keenness in A's desires, which, per-haps, is seldom known to be equally strong afterwards; so there are usually trials and exercises in B's experience, something different in their kind, and sharper in their measure, than what A was exposed to, or indeed had strength to endure. A, like Israel, has been delivered from Egypt by great power and a stretched-out arm, has been pursued and terrified by many enemies, has given himself up for lost again and again. He has at last seen his enemies destroyed, and has sung the song of Moses and the Lamb upon the banks of the Red Sea. Then he commences B. Perhaps, like Israel, he thinks his diffi-culties are at an end, and expects to go on rejoicing till he enters the promised land. But, alas! his difficulties are in a manner but beginning; he has a wilderness before him, of which he is not aware. The Lord is now about to suit his dis-pensations to humble and to prove him, and to show him what is in his heart, that he may do him good at the latter end, and that all the glory may redound to his own free grace.

Since the Lord hates and abhors sin, and teaches his people whom he loves to hate it likewise, it might seem desirable (and all things are equally easy to him), that at the same time they are delivered from the guilt and reigning power of sin, they should likewise be perfectly freed from the defilement of in-dwelling sin, and be made fully conformable to him at once. His wisdom has, however, appointed otherwise. But from the above premises, of his hatred of sin, and his love to his people, I think we may certainly conclude, that he would not suffer sin to remain in them, if he did not purpose to over-rule it, for the fuller manifestation of the glory of his grace and wis-dom, and for the making his salvation more precious to their

souls. It is, however, his command, and therefore their duty;
yea, further, from the new nature he has given them, it is their
desire to watch and strive against sin; and to propose the mor-
tification of the whole body of sin, and the advancement of
sanctification in their hearts, as their great and constant aim,
to which they are to have an habitual persevering regard.
Upon this plan B sets out. The knowledge of our acceptance
with God, and of our everlasting security in Christ, has in
itself the same tendency upon earth as it will have in heaven,
and would, in proportion to the degree of evidence and clear-
ness, produce the same effects of continual love, joy, peace,
gratitude, and praise, if there was nothing to counteract it.
But B is not all spirit. A depraved nature still cleaves to him,
and he has the seeds of every natural corruption yet remaining in his heart. He lives likewise in a world that is full of
snares and occasions, suited to draw forth those corruptions;
and he is surrounded by invisible spiritual enemies, the extent
of whose power and subtilty he is yet to learn by painful experience. B knows, in general, the nature of his Christian
warfare, and sees his right to live upon Jesus for righteousness
and strength. He is not unwilling to endure hardships as a
good soldier of Jesus Christ; and believes, that though he may
be sore thrust at that he may fall, the Lord will be his stay.
He knows that his heart is "deceitful and desperately
wicked;" but he does not, he cannot know at first the full
meaning of that expression. Yet it is for the Lord's glory, and
will in the end make his grace and love still more precious,
that B should find new and mortifying proofs of an evil
nature as he goes on, such as he could not once have believed
had they been foretold to him, as in the case of Peter, Mark
xiv. 29. And, in effect, the abominations of the heart do not
appear in their full strength and aggravation, but in the case
of one, who, like B, has tasted that the Lord is gracious, and
rejoiced in his salvation. The exceeding sinfulness of sin is
manifested, not so much by its breaking through the restraint
of threatenings and commands, as by its being capable of acting against light and against love. Thus it was with Hezekiah.
He had been a faithful and zealous servant of the Lord for
many years; but I suppose he knew more of God, and of him-

self, in the time of his sickness, than he had ever done before. The Lord, who had signally defended him from Sennacherib, was pleased likewise to raise him from the borders of the grave by a miracle, and prolonged the time of his life in answer to prayer. It is plain, from the song which he penned upon his recovery, that he was greatly affected with the mercies he had received: yet still there was something in his heart which he knew not, and which it was for the Lord's glory he should be made sensible of; and therefore he was pleased to leave him to himself. It is the only instance in which he is said to have been left to himself, and the only instance in which his conduct is condemned. I apprehend, that in the state of B, that is, for a season after we have known the Lord, we have usually the most sensible and distressing experience of our evil natures. I do not say, that it is necessary that we should be left to fall into gross outward sin, in order to know what is in our hearts; though I believe many have thus fallen, whose hearts, under a former sense of redeeming love, have been as truly set against sin, as the hearts of others who have been preserved from such outward falls. The Lord makes some of his children examples and warnings to others, as he pleases. They who are spared, and whose worst deviations are only known to the Lord and themselves, have great reason to be thankful. I am sure I have: the merciful Lord has not suffered me to make any considerable blot in my profession during the time I have been numbered amongst his people. But I have nothing to boast of herein. It has not been owing to my wisdom, watchfulness, or spirituality, though in the main he has not suffered me to live in the neglect of his appointed means. But I hope to go softly all my days under the remembrance of many things, for which I have as great cause to be abased before him, as if I had been left to sin grievously in the sight of men. Yet, with respect to my acceptance in the Beloved, I know not if I have had a doubt of a quarter of an hour's continuance for many years past. But, oh! the multiplied instances of stupidity, ingratitude, impatience, and rebellion, to which my conscience has been witness! And as every heart knows its own bitterness, I have generally heard the like complaints from others of the Lord's people with whom I have conversed, even from those who have appeared to be eminently gracious and spiritual. B does not meet with these things perhaps at first, nor every day. The Lord appoints occasions and turns in life, which try our spirits. There are particular seasons when temptations are suited to our frames, tempers, and situations; and there are times when he is pleased to withdraw, and to permit Satan's approach, that we may feel how vile we are in ourselves. We are prone to spiritual pride, to self-dependence, to vain confidence, to creature attachments, and a train of evils. The Lord often discovers to us one sinful disposition by exposing us to another. He sometimes shows us what he can do for us and in us; and at other times how little we can do, and how unable we are to stand without him. By a variety of these exercises, through the over-ruling and edifying influences of the Holy Spirit, B is trained up in a growing knowledge of himself and of the Lord. He learns to be more distrustful of his own heart, and to suspect a snare in every step he takes. The dark and disconsolate hours which he has brought upon himself in times past, make him doubly prize the light of God's countenance, and teach him to dread whatever might grieve the Spirit of God, and cause him to withdraw again. The repeated and multiplied pardons which he has received, increase his admiration of, and the sense of his obligations to, the rich sovereign abounding mercy of the covenant. Much has been forgiven him, therefore he loves much, and therefore he knows how to forgive and pity others. He does not call evil good, or good evil; but his own experiences teach him tenderness and forbearance. He experiences a spirit of meekness towards those who are overtaken in a fault, and his attempts to restore such, are according to the pattern of the Lord's dealings with himself. In a word, B's character, in my judgement, is complete, and he becomes a C, when the habitual frame of his heart answers to that passage in the prophet Ezekiel, chap. xvi. 63. "That thou mayest remember, and be confounded, and never open thy mouth any more (to boast, complain, or censure), because of thy shame, when I am pacified towards thee for all that thou hast done, saith the Lord God."

I am, &c.

LETTER III

C; *or, The full Corn in the Ear.*   Mark iv. 28.

Dear Sir,

BY way of distinction, I assigned to A the characteristic of *desire*, to B that of *conflict*. I can think of no single word more descriptive of the state of C than *contemplation*. His eminence, in comparison of A, does not consist in the *sensible* warmth and fervency of his affections: in this respect many of the most exemplary believers have looked back with a kind of regret upon the time of their espousals, when, though their judgements were but imperfectly formed, and their views of Gospel-truths were very indistinct, they felt a fervour of spirit, the remembrance of which is both humbling and refreshing; and yet they cannot recall the same sensations. Nor is he properly distinguished from B by a consciousness of his acceptance in the Beloved, and an ability of calling God his Father; for this I have supposed B has attained to. Though as there is a growth in every grace, C having had his views of the Gospel, and of the Lord's faithfulness and mercy, confirmed by a longer experience, his assurance is of course more *stable* and more *simple*, than when he first saw himself safe from all condemnation. Neither has C, properly speaking, any more strength or stock of grace inherent in himself than B, or even than A. He is in the same state of absolute dependence, as incapable of performing spiritual acts, or of resisting temptations by his own power, as he was at the first day of his setting out. Yet in a sense he is much stronger, because he has a more feeling and constant sense of his own weakness. The Lord has been long teaching him this lesson by a train of various dispensations; and through grace he can say, he has not suffered so many things in vain. His heart has deceived him so often, that he is now in a good measure weaned from trusting to it; and therefore he does not meet with so many disappointments. And having found again and again the vanity of all other helps, he is now taught to go to the Lord *at once* for "grace to help in every time of need." Thus he is strong, not in himself, but in the grace that is in Christ Jesus.

But C's happiness and superiority to B lies chiefly in this, that by the Lord's blessing on the use of means, such as prayer, reading and hearing of the word, and by a sanctified improvement of what he has seen of the Lord, and of his own heart, in the course of his experience, he has attained clearer, deeper, and more comprehensive views of the mystery of redeeming love; of the glorious excellency of the Lord Jesus, in his person, offices, grace, and faithfulness; of the harmony and glory of all the divine perfections manifested in and by him to the church; of the stability, beauty, fulness, and certainty of the Holy Scriptures, and of the heights, depths, lengths, and breadths of the love of God in Christ. Thus though his sensible feelings may not be so warm as when he was in the state of A, his judgement is more solid, his mind more fixed, his thoughts more habitually exercised upon the things within the veil. His great business is to behold the glory of God in Christ; and by beholding, he is changed into the same image, and brings forth in an eminent and uniform manner the fruits of righteousness, which are by Jesus Christ to the glory and praise of God. His contemplations are not barren speculations, but have a real influence, and enable him to exemplify the Christian character to more advantage, and with more consistence, than can in the present state of things be expected either from A or B. The following particulars may illustrate my meaning.

I. Humility. A measure of this grace is to be expected in every true Christian: but it can only appear in proportion to the knowledge they have of Christ and of their own hearts. It is a part of C's daily employment to look back upon the way by which the Lord has led him; and while he reviews the *Ebenezers* he has set up all along the road, he sees, in almost an equal number, the monuments of his own perverse returns, and how he has in a thousand instances rendered to the Lord evil for good. Comparing these things together, he can without affectation adopt the apostle's language, and style himself "less than the least of all saints, and of sinners the chief." A and B know that they ought to be humbled; but C is truly so, and feels the force of that text which I mentioned in my last; Ezek. xvi. 63. Again, as he knows most of himself, so he has seen most of the Lord. The apprehension of infinite Majesty combined with infinite love, makes him shrink into the dust. From the exercise of this grace he derives two others, which are exceedingly ornamental, and principal branches of the mind which was in Christ.

The one is, submission to the will of God. The views he has of his own vileness, unworthiness, and ignorance, and of the divine sovereignty, wisdom, and love, teach him to be content in every state, and to bear his appointed lot of suffering with resignation, according to the language of David in a time of affliction, "I was dumb, and opened not my mouth, because thou didst it."

The other is, tenderness of spirit towards his fellow Christians. He cannot but judge of their conduct according to the rule of the word. But his own heart, and the knowledge he has acquired of the snares of the world, and the subtilty of Satan, teach him to make all due allowances, and qualify him for admonishing and restoring, in the spirit of meekness, those who have been overtaken in a fault. Here A is usually blameable; the warmth of his zeal, not being duly corrected by a sense of his own imperfections, betrays him often into a censorious spirit. But C can bear with A likewise, because he hath been so himself, and he will not expect green fruit to be ripe.

II. Spirituality. A spiritual taste, and a disposition to account all things mean and vain, in comparison of the knowledge and love of God in Christ, are essential to a true Christian. The world can never be his prevailing choice; 1 John ii. 15. Yet we are renewed but in part, and are prone to an undue attachment to worldly things. Our spirits cleave to the dust, in defiance to the dictates of our better judgements; and I believe the Lord seldom gives his people a considerable victory over this evil principle, until he has let them feel how deeply it is rooted in their hearts. We may often see persons entangled and clogged in this respect, of whose sincerity in the main we cannot justly doubt; especially upon some sudden and unexpected turn in life, which brings them into a situation they have not been accustomed to. A considerable part of our trials are mercifully appointed to wean us from this propensity; and it is gradually weakened by the Lord's showing us at one time the vanity of the creature, and at another his own excellence and all-sufficiency. Even C is not perfect in this respect; but he is more sensible of the evil of such attachments, more humbled for them, more watchful against them, and more delivered from them. He still feels a fetter, but he longs to be free. His allowed desires are brought to a point; and he sees nothing worth a serious thought but communion with God and progress in holiness. Whatever outward changes C may meet with, he will in general be the same màn still. He has learned with the apostle, not only to suffer want, but (which is perhaps the harder lesson) how to abound. A palace would be a prison to him without the Lord's presence, and with this a prison would be a palace. From hence arises a peaceful reliance upon the Lord; he has nothing which he cannot commit into his hands, which he is not habitually aiming to resign to his disposal. Therefore he is not afraid of evil tidings; but when the hearts of others shake like the leaves of a tree, he is fixed, trusting in the Lord, who he believes *can* and *will* make good every loss, sweeten every bitter, and appoint all things to work together for his advantage. He sees that the time is short, lives upon the foretastes of glory, and therefore accounts not his life, or any inferior concernment, dear, so that he may finish his course with joy.

III. A union of heart to the glory and will of God, is another noble distinction of C's spirit. The glory of God and the good of his people are inseparably connected. But of these great ends the first is unspeakably the highest and the most important, and into which everything else will be finally resolved. Now, in proportion as we advance nearer to him, *our* judgement, aim, and end, will be conformable to *his*, and his glory will have the highest place in our hearts. At first it is not so, or but very imperfectly. Our concern is chiefly about ourselves; nor can it be otherwise. The convinced soul inquires, What shall I do to be saved? The young convert is

intent upon sensible comforts; and in the seasons when he sees
his interest secure, the prospect of the troubles he may meet
with in life makes him often wish for an early dismission, that
he may be at rest, and avoid the heat and burden of the day.
But C has attained to more enlarged views; he has a desire to
depart and to be with Christ, which would be importunate if
he considered only himself; but his chief desire is, that God
may be glorified in him, whether by his life or by his death.
He is not his own; nor does he desire to be his own; but so
that the power of Jesus may be manifested in him, he will take
pleasure in infirmities, in distresses, in temptations; and though
he longs for heaven, would be content to live as long as Methu-
selah upon earth, if, by any thing he could do or suffer, the
will and glory of God might be promoted. And though he loves
and adores the Lord for what he has done and suffered for
him, delivered him from, and appointed him to; yet he loves
and adores him likewise with a more simple and direct love,
in which self is in a manner forgot, from the consideration of
his glorious excellence and perfections, as he is in himself.
That God in Christ is glorious over all, and blessed for ever,
is the very joy of his soul; and his heart can frame no higher
wish, than that the sovereign, wise, holy will of God may be
accomplished in him, and all his creatures. Upon this grand
principle his prayers, schemes, and actions, are formed. Thus
C is already made like the angels; and, so far as is consistent
with the inseparable remnants of a fallen nature, the will of
God is regarded by him upon earth, as it is by the inhabitants
of heaven.

The power of divine grace in C may be exemplified in a great
variety of situations. C may be rich or poor, learned or illit-
erate, of a lively natural spirit, or of a more slow and phleg-
matical constitution. He may have a comparatively smooth,
or a remarkably thorny path in life; he may be a minister or
layman; these circumstantials will give some tincture and difference in appearance to the work; but the work itself is the
same; and we must, as far as possible, drop the consideration
of them all, or make proper allowances for each, in order to
form a right judgement of the life of faith. The outward expression of grace may be heightened and set off to advantage

by many things which are merely natural, such as evenness of temper, good sense, a knowledge of the world, and the like; and it may be darkened by things which are not properly sinful, but unavoidable, such as lowness of spirit, weak abilities, and pressure of temptations, which may have effects that they who have not had experience in the same things cannot properly account for. A double quantity of real grace, if I may so speak, that has a double quantity of hindrances to conflict with, will not be easily observed, unless these hindrances are likewise known and attended to; and a smaller measure of grace may appear great when its exercise meets with no remarkable obstruction. For these reasons, we can never be competent judges of each other, because we cannot be competently acquainted with the whole complex case. But our great and merciful High-priest knows the whole; he considers our frame, " remembers that we are but dust;" makes gracious allowances, pities, bears, accepts, and approves, with unerring judgement. The sun, in his daily course,, beholds nothing so excellent and honourable upon earth as C, though perhaps he may be confined to a cottage, and is little known or noticed by men. But he is the object and residence of divine love, the charge of angels, and ripening for everlasting glory. Happy C! his toils, sufferings, and exercises, will be soon at an end; soon his desires will be accomplished; and he who has loved him, and redeemed him with his own blood, will receive him to himself, with a " Well done, good and faithful servant; enter thou into the joy of thy Lord."

If this representation is agreeable to the Scriptures, how greatly are they mistaken, and how much to be pitied, who, while they make profession of the Gospel, seem to have no idea of the effects it is designed to produce upon the hearts of believers, but either allow themselves in a worldly spirit and conversation, or indulge their unsanctified tempers, by a fierce contention for names, notions, and parties. May the Lord give to you and to me daily to grow in the experience of that wisdom which " is first pure, then peaceable, gentle, and easy to be intreated, full of mercy and good works, without partiality, and without hypocrisy."

I am, &c,

LETTER IV

Communion with God.

Dear Sir,

THOUGH many authors have written largely and well concerning communion with God, I shall not refer you to books, or have recourse to them myself; but, in compliance with your request, shall simply offer you what occurs to my thoughts upon the subject. I propose not to exceed the limits of a sheet of paper, and must therefore come immediately to the point.

That God is to be worshipped, is generally acknowledged; but that they who worship him in spirit, and in truth, have real fellowship and communion with him, is known only to themselves. The world can neither understand nor believe it. Many who would not be thought to have cast off all reverence for the Scripture, and therefore do not choose flatly to contradict the apostle's testimony, 1 John i. 3, attempt to evade its force by restraining it to the primitive times. They will allow that it might be so then; but they pretend that circumstances with us are greatly altered. Circumstances are, indeed, altered with us, so far, that men may now pass for Christians who confess and manifest themselves strangers to the Spirit of Christ: but who can believe that the very nature and design of Christianity should alter in the course of time? and that communion with God, which was essential to it in the apostle's days, should be now so unnecessary and impracticable, as to expose all who profess an acquaintance with it to the charge of enthusiasm and folly? However, they who have tasted that the Lord is gracious, will not be disputed out of their spiritual senses. If they are competent judges whether they ever saw the light, or felt the beams of the sun, they are no less certain that, by the knowledge of the Gospel, they are brought into a state of communion with God.

Communion presupposes union. By nature we are strangers, yea, enemies to God; but we are reconciled, brought nigh, and become his children, by faith in Christ Jesus. We can have no true knowledge of God, desire towards him, access unto him, or gracious communications from him, but in and through the Son of his love. He is the medium of this inestimable privilege: for he is the way, the only way, of intercourse between heaven and earth; the sinner's way to God, and God's way of mercy to the sinner. If any pretend to know God, and to have communion with him, otherwise than by the knowledge of Jesus Christ, whom he hath sent, and by faith in his name, it is a proof that they neither know God nor themselves. God, if considered abstracted from the revelation of himself in the person of Jesus, is a consuming fire; and if he should look upon us without respect to his covenant of mercy established in the Mediator, we could expect nothing from him but indignation and wrath. But when his Holy Spirit enables us to receive the record which he has given of his Son, we are delivered and secured from condemnation; we are accepted in the Beloved; we are united to him in whom all the fulness of the Godhead substantially dwells, and all the riches of divine wisdom, power, and love, are treasured up. Thus in him, as the temple wherein the glory of God is manifested, and by him, as the representative and high priest of his people, and through him, as the living head of his mystical body the church, believers maintain communion with God. They have meat to eat which the world knows not of, honour which cometh of God only, joy which a stranger intermeddleth not with. They are for the most part poor and afflicted, frequently scorned and reproached, accounted hypocrites or visionaries, knaves or fools; but this one thing makes amends for all, " They have fellowship with the Father, and with his son Jesus Christ."

I would observe further, that as the incarnation of that Mighty one, on whom our help is laid, was necessary, that a perfect obedience to the law, and a complete and proper atonement for sin, might be accomplished in the human nature that had sinned, and fallen short of the glory of God; so, in another view, it affords us unspeakable advantage for our comfortable and intimate communion with God by him. The adorable and awful perfections of Deity are softened, if I may so speak, and rendered more familiar and engaging to our apprehensions, when we consider them as resident in him, who is very bone of our bone, and flesh of our flesh; and who, having by himself purged our sins, is now seated on the right hand of the Majesty on high, and reigns in the nature of man, over all, God blessed for ever. Thus he who knows our frame, by becoming man like ourselves, is the supreme and ultimate object of that phil-anthropy, that human affection, which he originally implanted in us. He has made us susceptive of the endearments of friend-ship and relative life; and he admits us to communion with himself under the most engaging characters and relations, as our friend, our brother, and our husband.

They who, by that faith which is of the operation of God, are thus united to him in Christ, are brought thereby into a state of real habitual communion with him. The degree of its exercise and sensible perception on our parts, is various in dif-ferent persons, and in the same person at different times; for it depends upon the communications we receive from the Lord, the Spirit, who distributes to every man severally according to his will, adjusting his dispensations with a wise and merciful respect to our present state of discipline. If we were wholly freed from the effects of a depraved nature, the snares of an evil world, and the subtle temptations of Satan, our actual communion with God would be always lively, sensible, and fervent. It will be thus in heaven; there its exercise will be without obstruction, abatement, or interruption. But so long as we are liable to security, spiritual pride, indolence, an un-due attachment to worldly things, and irregular distempered passions, the Lord is pleased to afford, increase, suspend, or renew, the sensible impressions of his love and grace, in such seasons and measures as he sees most suitable to prevent or control these evils, or to humble us for them. We grieve his Spirit, and he withdraws; but, by his secret power over our hearts, he makes us sensible of our folly and loss, teaches us to mourn after him, and to entreat his return. These desires, which are the effects of his own grace, he answers in his own time, and shines forth upon the soul with healing in his beams. But such is our weakness, and so unapt are we to retain even those lessons which we have learnt by painful experience, that we are prone to repeat our former miscarriages, and to render a repetition of the same changes necessary. From hence it is that what we call our *frames* are so very variable, and that our comfortable sense of divine communion is rather transient than abiding. But the communion itself, upon which the life and safety of our souls depend, is never totally obstructed; nor can it be, unless God should be unmindful of his covenant, and forsake the work of his own hands. And when it is not perceptible to sense, it may ordinarily be made evident to faith, by duly comparing what we read in the Scripture with what passes in our hearts. I say *ordinarily*, because there may be some excepted cases. If a believer is unhappily brought under the power of some known sin, or has grievously and notoriously declined from his profession, it is possible that the Lord may hide himself behind so dark a cloud, and leave him for a while to such hardness of heart, as that he shall seem to himself to be utterly destitute and forsaken. And the like apprehensions may be formed under some of Satan's violent temptations, when he is permitted to come in as a flood, and to overpower the apparent exercise of every grace by a torrent of blasphemous and evil imaginations. Yet the Lord is still present with his people in the darkest hours, or the unavoidable event of such cases would be apostasy or despair. Psalm xli. 11.

The communion we speak of comprises a mutual intercourse and communication in love, in counsels, and in interests.

In love. The Lord, by his Spirit, manifests and confirms his love to his people. For this purpose he meets them at his throne of grace, and in his ordinances. There he makes himself known unto them, as he does not unto the world; causes his goodness to pass before them; opens, applies, and seals to them his exceeding great and precious promises; and gives them the Spirit of adoption, whereby, unworthy as they are, they are enabled to cry, " Abba, Father." He causes them to understand that great love wherewith he has loved them, in redeeming them by price and by power, washing them from their sins in the blood of the Lamb, recovering them from the dominion of Satan, and preparing for them an everlasting kingdom, where they shall see his face, and rejoice in his glory. The knowledge of this his love to them, produces a return of love from them to him. They adore him, and admire him; they make an unreserved surrender of their hearts to him. They view him and delight in him as their God, their Saviour, and their portion. They account his favour better than life. He is the sun of their souls: if he is pleased to shine upon them, all is well, and they are not greatly careful about other things; but if he hides his face, the smiles of the whole creation can afford them no solid comfort. They esteem one day or hour spent in the delightful contemplation of his glorious excellencies, and in the expression of their desires towards him, better than a thousand; and when their love is most fervent, they are ashamed that it is so faint, and chide and bemoan themselves that they can love him no more. This often makes them long to depart, willing to leave their dearest earthly comforts, that they may see him as he is, without a vail or cloud; for they know that then, and not till then, they shall love him as they ought.

In counsels. The secret of the Lord is with them that fear him. He deals familiarly with them. He calls them not servants only, but friends; and he treats them as friends. He affords them more than promises; for he opens to them the plan of his great designs from everlasting to everlasting; shows them the strong foundations and inviolable securities of his favour towards them, the height, and depth, and length, and breadth of his love, which passeth knowledge, and the unsearchable riches of his grace. He instructs them in the mysterious conduct of his providence, the reasons and ends of all his dispensations in which they are concerned; and solves a thousand hard questions to their satisfaction, which are inexplicable to the natural wisdom of man. He teaches them likewise the beauty of his precepts, the path of their duty, and the nature of their warfare. He acquaints them with the plots of their enemies, the snares and dangers they are exposed to, and the best methods of avoiding them. And he permits and enables them to acquaint him with all their cares, fears, wants, and troubles, with more freedom than they can unbosom themselves to their nearest earthly friends. His ear is always open to them; he is never weary of hearing their complaints, and

answering their petitions. The men of the world would account
it a high honour and privilege to have an unrestrained liberty of
access to an earthly king; but what words can express the privilege and honour of believers, who, whenever they please, have
audience of the King of kings, whose compassion, mercy, and
power are, like his majesty, infinite. The world wonders at
their indifference to the vain pursuits and amusements by
which others are engrossed; that they are so patient in trouble,
so inflexible in their conduct, so well satisfied with that state of
poverty and obscurity which the Lord, for the most part, allots
them, but the wonder would cease if what passes in secret
were publicly known. They have obtained the pearl of great
price; they have communion with God; they derive their wisdom, strength and comfort from on high, and cast all their
cares upon him who, they assuredly know, vouchsafes to take
care of them. This reminds me of another branch of their
communion, namely,

In interests. The Lord claims them for his portion, he
accounts them his jewels, and their happiness in time and
eternity is the great end which, next to his own glory, and in
inseparable connexion with it, he has immediately and invariably in view. In this point all his dispensations of grace and
providence shall finally terminate. He himself is their guide
and their guard; he keeps them as the apple of his eye; the
hairs of their head are numbered, and not an event in their
lives takes place but in an appointed subserviency to their final
good. And as he is pleased to espouse *their* interest, they
through grace, are devoted to *his*. They are no longer their
own, they *would not* be their own; it is their desire, their joy,
their glory, to live to him who died for them. He has won
their hearts by his love, and made them a willing people in the
day of his power. The glory of his name, the success of his
cause, the prosperity of his people, the accomplishment of his
will, these are the great and leading objects which are engraven
upon their hearts, and to which all their prayers, desires, and
endeavours, are directed. They would count nothing dear,
not even their lives, if set in competition with these. In the
midst of their afflictions, if the Lord is glorified, if sinners are
converted, if the church flourishes, they can rejoice. But when

iniquity abounds, when love waxes cold, when professors depart from the doctrines of truth, and the power of godliness, then they are grieved and pained to the heart; then they are touched in what they account their nearest interest, because it is their Lord's.

This is the spirit of a true Christian. May the Lord increase it in us, and in all who love his name! I have room only to subscribe myself, &c.

LETTER V

Spiritual Blindness.

Dear Sir,

THE question, What is the discriminating characteristic nature of a work of grace upon the soul? has been upon my mind; if I am able to give you satisfaction concerning it, I shall think my time well employed.

The reason why men in a natural state are utterly ignorant of spiritual truths is, that they are wholly destitute of a faculty suited to their perception. A remarkable instance we have in the absurd construction which Nicodemus put upon what our Lord had spoken to him concerning the new birth. And in the supernatural communication of this spiritual faculty, by the agency of the Holy Spirit, I apprehend the inimitable and abiding criterion, which is the subject of our inquiry, does primarily consist. Those passages of Scripture wherein the Gospel-truth is compared to light, lead to a familiar illustration of my meaning. Men by nature are stark blind with respect to this light; by grace the eyes of the understanding are opened. Among a number of blind men, some may be more ingenious and of better capacity than others. They may be better qualified for such studies and employments which do not require eyesight than many who can see, and may attain to considerable skill in them; but with respect to the true nature of light and colours,

they are all exactly upon a level. A blind man, if ingenious
and inquisitive, may learn to talk about the light, the sun, or
the rainbow, in terms borrowed from those who have seen
them; but it is impossible that he can have (I mean a man born
blind) a just idea of either; and whatever hearsay-knowledge he
may have acquired, he can hardly talk much upon these subjects without betraying his real ignorance. The case of one
mentioned by Mr. Locke has been often quoted. He believed,
that after much inquiry and reflection, he had at last found
out what scarlet was; and being asked to explain himself, " I
think," says he, " scarlet is something like the sound of a
trumpet." This man had about the same knowledge of natural
light as Nicodemus had of spiritual. Nor can all the learning
or study in the world enable any person to form a suitable
judgement of divine truth, till the eyes of his mind are opened,
and then he will perceive it at once.

Indeed this comparison is well suited to show the entire difference between nature and grace, and to explain the ground
of that enmity and scorn which fills the hearts of blinded
sinners, against those who profess to have been enlightened
by the Spirit of God. The reason why blind men are not
affronted when we tell them they cannot see, seems to be, that
they are borne down by the united testimony of all who are
about them. Every one talks of seeing; and they find by
experience, that those who say they can see can do many
things which the blind cannot. Some such conviction as this
many have, who live where the Gospel is preached, and is
made the power of God to the salvation of others. The conversation and conduct of the people of God convinces them,
that there is a difference, though they cannot tell wherein it
consists. But if we could suppose it possible, that there was
a whole nation of blind men, and one or two persons should
go amongst them, and profess that they could see, while they
could not offer them such a proof of their assertion as they
were capable of receiving, nor even explain, to their satisfaction, what they meant by sight; what may we imagine would
be the consequence? I think there is little doubt but these
innovators would experience much the same treatment as the
believers of Jesus often meet with from a blind world. The

blind people would certainly hate and despise them for presuming to pretend to what *they* had not. They would try to dispute them out of their senses, and bring many arguments to prove, that there could be no such thing as either light or sight. They would say, as many say now, How is it, if these things are so, that *we* should know nothing of them? Yea, I think it probable, they would rise against them as deceivers and enthusiasts, and disturbers of the public peace, and say, " Away with such fellows from the earth; it is not fit that they should live." But if we should suppose further, that during the heat of the contest some of these blind men should have their eyes suddenly opened, the dispute as to them would be at an end in a minute; they would confess their former ignorance and obstinacy, confirm the testimony of those whom they had before despised, and of course share in the same treatment from their blind brethren, perhaps be treated still worse, as apostates from the opinion of the public.

If this illustration is justly applicable to our subject, it may lead us to several observations, or inferences, which have a tendency to confirm what we are elsewhere expressly taught by the word of God.

In the first place, it shows, that regeneration, or that great change without which a man cannot see the kingdom of God, is the effect of Almighty power. Neither education, endeavours, nor arguments, can open the eyes of the blind. It is God alone, who at first caused light to shine out of darkness, who can shine into our hearts, " to give us the light of the knowledge of the glory of God in the face of Jesus Christ." People may attain some natural ideas of spiritual truths by reading books, or hearing sermons, and may thereby become wise in their own conceits; they may learn to imitate the language of an experienced Christian; but they know not what they say, nor whereof they affirm, and are as distant from the true meaning of the terms, as a blind man, who pronounces the words *blue* or *red*, is from the ideas which those words raise in the mind of a person who can distinguish colours by his sight. And from hence we may infer the sovereignty, as well as the efficacy, of grace; since it is evident, not only that the objective light, the word of God, is not afforded universally to all men; but that those who enjoy the same outward means, have not all the same perceptions. There are many who stumble in the noon-day, not for want of light, but for want of eyes; and they who now see were once blind even as others, and had neither power nor will to enlighten their own minds. It is a mercy, however, when people are so far sensible of their own blindness, as to be willing to wait for the manifestation of the Lord's power, in the ordinances of his own appointment. He came into the world, and he sends forth his Gospel, that those who see not may see; and when there is a desire in the heart for spiritual sight, it shall in his due time be answered.

From hence likewise we may observe the proper use and value of the preaching of the Gospel, which is the great instrument by which the Holy Spirit opens the blind eyes. Like the rod of Moses, it owes all its efficacy to the appointment and promise of God. Ministers cannot be too earnest in the discharge of their office; it behoves them to use all diligence to find out acceptable words, and to proclaim the whole counsel of God. Yet when they have done all, they have done nothing, unless their word is accompanied to the heart by the power and demonstration of the Spirit. Without this blessing, an apostle might labour in vain; but it shall be in a measure afforded to all who preach the truth in love, in simplicity, and in an humble dependence upon him who alone can give success. This in a great measure puts all faithful ministers on a level, notwithstanding any seeming disparity in gifts and abilities. Those who have a lively and pathetic talent, may engage the ear, and raise the natural passions of their hearers; but they cannot reach the heart. The blessing may be rather expected to attend the humble than the voluble speaker.

Further we may remark, that there is a difference in kind, between the highest attainments of nature, and the effects of grace in the lowest degree. Many are convinced, who are not truly enlightened; are afraid of the consequences of sin, though they never saw its evil; have a seeming desire of salvation, which is not founded upon a truly spiritual discovery of their own wretchedness, and the excellency of Jesus. These may, for a season, hear the word with joy, and walk in the way of professors; but we need not be surprised if they do not hold out, for they have no root. Though many such fall, the foundation of God still standeth sure. We may confidently affirm, upon the warrant of Scripture, that they who, having for a while escaped the pollutions of the world, are again habitually entangled in them, or who, having been distressed upon the account of sin, can find relief in a self-righteous course, and stop short of Christ, " who is the end of the law for righteousness to every one that believeth;" we may affirm, that these, whatever profession they may have made, were never capable of receiving the beauty and glory of the Gospel-salvation. On the other hand, though, where the eyes are divinely enlightened, the soul's first views of itself and of the Gospel may be confused and indistinct, like him who saw men as it were trees walking: yet this light is like the dawn, which, though weak and faint at its first appearance, shineth more and more unto the perfect day. It is the work of God; and his work is perfect in kind, though progressive in the manner. He will not despise or forsake the day of small things. When he thus begins, he will make an end; and such persons, however feeble, poor, and worthless, in their own apprehensions, if they have obtained a glimpse of the Redeemer's glory, as he is made unto us, of God, wisdom, righteousness, sanctification, and redemption, so that his name is precious, and the desire of their hearts is towards him, have good reason to hope and believe, as the wife of Manoah did in a similar case, that if the Lord had been pleased to kill them he would not have showed them such things as these.

Once more: This spiritual sight and faculty is that which may be principally considered as inherent in a believer. He has no stock of grace, or comfort, or strength, in himself. He needs continual supplies; and if the Lord withdraws from him, he is as weak and unskilful, after he has been long engaged in the Christian warfare, as he was when he first entered upon it. The eye is of little present use in the dark; for it cannot see without light. But the return of light is no advantage to a blind man. A believer may be much in the dark; but his spiritual sight remains. Though the exercise of grace may be low, he knows himself, he knows the Lord, he knows the way of access to a throne of grace. His frames and feelings may

alter; but he has received such a knowledge of the person and
offices, the power and grace, of Jesus the Saviour, as cannot
be taken from him; and he could withstand even an angel that
should preach another gospel, because he has *seen* the Lord.
The paper constrains me to break off. May the Lord increase
his light in your heart, and in the heart of, &c.

LETTER VI

The Right Use of the Law.

Dear Sir,

You desire my thoughts on 1 Tim. i. 8. " We know the law
is good, if a man use it lawfully," and I willingly comply. I
do not mean to send you a sermon on the text; yet a little attention to method may not be improper upon this subject, though
in a letter to a friend. Ignorance of the nature and design of
the law is at the bottom of most religious mistakes. This is the
root of self-righteousness, the grand reason why the Gospel of
Christ is no more regarded, and the cause of that uncertainty
and inconsistency in many, who, though they profess themselves teachers, understand not what they say, nor whereof
they affirm. If we previously state what is meant by the law,
and by what means we know the law to be good, I think it will,
from these premises, be easy to conclude what it is to use the
law *lawfully*.

The law, in many passages of the Old Testament, signifies
the whole revelation of the will of God, as in Psalm i. 2 and
xix. 7. But the law, in a strict sense, is contradistinguished
from the Gospel. Thus the apostle considers it at large in his
epistles to the Romans and Galatians. I think it evident, that,
in the passage you have proposed, the apostle is speaking of
the law of Moses. But, to have a clearer view of the subject,
it may be proper to look back to a more early period.

The law of God, then, in the largest sense, is that rule, or prescribed course, which he has appointed for his creatures according to their several natures and capacities, that they may answer the end for which he has created them. Thus it comprehends the inanimate creation. The wind or storm fulfil his word or law. He hath appointed the moon for its seasons; and the sun knoweth its going down, or going forth, and performs all its revolutions according to its Maker's pleasure. If we could suppose the sun was an intelligent being, and should refuse to shine, or should wander from the station in which God had placed it, it would then be a transgressor of the law. But there is no such disorder in the natural world. The law of God in this sense, or what many choose to call the law of nature, is no other than the impression of God's power, whereby all things continue and act according to his will from the beginning: for "he spake, and it was done; he commanded, and it stood fast."

The animals destitute of reason are likewise under a law; that is, God has given them instincts according to their several kinds, for their support and preservation, to which they invariably conform. A wisdom unspeakably superior to all the contrivance of man disposes their concernments, and is visible in the structure of a bird's nest, or the economy of a bee-hive. But this wisdom is restrained within narrow limits; they act without any remote design, and are incapable either of good or evil in a moral sense.

When God created man, he taught him more than the beasts of the earth, and made him wiser than the fowls of heaven. He formed him for himself, breathed into him a spirit immortal and incapable of dissolution, gave him a capacity not to be satisfied with any creature good, endued him with an understanding, will, and affections, which qualified him for the knowledge and service of his Maker, and a life of communion with him. The law of God, therefore, concerning man, is that rule of disposition and conduct to which a creature so constituted ought to conform; so that the end of his creation might be answered, and the wisdom of God be manifested in him and by him. Man's continuance in this regular and happy state was not necessary as it is in the creatures, who, having no rational faculties, have properly no choice, but act under the immediate agency of divine power. As man was capable of continuing in the state in which he was created, so he was capable of forsaking it. He did so, and sinned by eating the forbidden fruit. We are not to suppose that this prohibition was the whole of the law of Adam, so that if he had abstained from the tree of knowledge, he might in other respects have done (as we say) what he pleased. This injunction was the test of his obedience; and while he regarded it, he could have no desire contrary to holiness, because his nature was holy. But when he broke through it, he broke through the whole law, and stood guilty of idolatry, blasphemy, rebellion, and murder. The divine light in his soul was extinguished, the image of God defaced; he became like Satan, whom he had obeyed, and lost his power to keep that law which was connected with his happiness. Yet still the law remained in force: the blessed God could not lose his right to that reverence, love, and obedience, which must always be due to him from his intelligent creatures. Thus Adam became a transgressor, and incurred the penalty, death. But God, who is rich in mercy, according to his eternal purpose revealed the promise of the seed of the woman, and instituted sacrifices as types of that atonement for sin, which *He* in the fulness of time should accomplish by the sacrifice of himself.

Adam, after his fall, was no longer a public person, he was saved by grace, through faith: but the depravity he had brought upon human nature remained. His children, and so all his posterity, were born in his sinful likeness, without either ability or inclination to keep the law. The earth was soon filled with violence. But a few in every successive age were preserved by grace, and faith in the promise. Abraham was favoured with a more full and distinct revelation of the covenant of grace; he saw the day of Christ, and rejoiced. In the time of Moses, God was pleased to set apart a peculiar people to himself, and to them he published his law with great solemnity at Sinai: this law consisted of two distinct parts, very different in their scope and design, though both enjoined by the same authority.

The decalogue, or ten commands, uttered by the voice of God himself, is an abstract of that original law under which man was created, but published in a prohibitory form, the Israelites, like the rest of mankind, being depraved by sin, and strongly inclined to the commission of every evil. This law could not be designed as a covenant, by obedience to which man should be justified; for long before its publication the Gospel had been preached to Abraham, Gal. iii. 8. But the law entered that sin might abound; that the extent, the evil, and the desert of sin might be known; for it reaches to the most hidden thoughts of the heart, requires absolute and perpetual obedience, and denounces a curse upon all who continue not therein.

To this was superadded the ceremonial or Levitical law, prescribing a variety of institutions, purifications, and sacrifices; the observance of which were, during that dispensation, absolutely necessary to the acceptable worship of God. By obedience to these prescriptions, the people of Israel preserved their legal right to the blessings promised to them as a nation, and which were not confined to spiritual worshippers only: and they were likewise ordinances and helps to lead those who truly feared God, and had conscience of sin, to look forward by faith to the great sacrifice, the Lamb of God, who in the fulness of time was to take away sin by the sacrifice of himself. In both these respects the ceremonial law was abrogated by the death of Christ. The Jews then ceased to be God's peculiar people; and Jesus having expiated sin, and brought in an everlasting righteousness by his obedience unto death, all other sacrifices bcame unnecessary and vain. The Gospel supplies the place of the ceremonial law to the same advantage as the sun abundantly compensates for the twinkling of the stars, and the feeble glimmering of moon-light, which are concealed by its glory. Believers of old were relieved from the strictness of the moral law by the sacrifices which pointed to Christ. Believers under the Gospel are relieved by a direct application of the blood of the covenant. Both renounce any dependence on the moral law for justification, and both accept it as a rule of life in the hands of the Mediator, and are enabled to yield it a sincere, though not a perfect, obedience.

If an Israelite, trusting in his obedience to the moral law, had ventured to reject the ordinances of the ceremonial, he would have been cut off. In like manner, if any who are called Christians are so well satisfied with their moral duties, that they see no necessity of making Christ their only hope, the law by which they seek life will be to them a ministration unto death. Christ, and he alone, delivers us, by faith in his name, from the curse of the law, having been made a curse for us.

A second inquiry is, How we came to know the law to be good? For naturally we do not, we cannot think so. We cannot be at enmity with God, and at the same time approve of his law; rather this is the ground of our dislike to him, that we conceive the law by which we are to be judged is too strict in its precepts, and too severe in its threatenings; and therefore men, so far as in them lies, are for altering this law. They think it would be better if it required no more than we can perform, if it allowed us more liberty, and especially if it was not armed against transgressors with the penalty of everlasting punishment. This is evident from the usual pleas of un-awakened sinners: some think, "I am not so bad as some others"; by which they mean, God will surely make a difference, and take favourable notice of what they suppose good in themselves. Others plead, "If *I* should not obtain mercy, what will become of the greatest part of mankind?" by which they plainly intimate, that it would be hard and unjust in God to punish such multitudes. Others endeavour to extenuate their sins, as Jonathan once said, "I did but taste a little honey, and I must die." "These passions are natural to me, and must I die for indulging them?" In short, the spirituality and strictness of the law, its severity, and its levelling effect, con-founding all seeming differences in human characters, and stopping every mouth without distinction, are three properties of the law which the natural man cannot allow to be good.

These prejudices against the law can only be removed by the power of the Holy Spirit. It is his office to enlighten and convince the conscience; to communicate an impression of the majesty, holiness, justice, and authority of the God with whom we have to do, whereby the evil and desert of sin is apprehended: the sinner is then stripped of all his vain pretences, is compelled to plead guilty, and must justify his judge, even though he should condemn him. It is *his* office likewise to discover the grace and glory of the Saviour, as having fulfilled the law for us, and as engaged by promise to enable those who believe in him to honour it with a due obedience in their own persons. Then a change of judgement takes place, and the sinner consents to the law, that it is holy, just, and good. Then the law is acknowledged to be holy: it manifests the holiness of God; and a conformity to it is the perfection of human nature. There can be no excellence in man, but so far as he is influenced by God's law: without it, the greater his natural powers and abilities are, he is but so much the more detestable and mischievous. It is assented to as just, springing from his indubitable right and authority over his creatures, and suited to their dependence upon him, and the abilities with which he originally endowed them. And though we by sin have lost those abilities, his right remains unalienable; and therefore he can justly punish transgressors. And as it is just in respect to God, so it is good for man; his obedience to the law, and the favour of God therein, being his proper happiness, and it is impossible for him to be happy in any other way. Only, as I have hinted, to sinners these things must be applied according to the Gospel, and to their new relation by faith to the Lord Jesus Christ, who has obeyed the law, and made atonement for sin on their behalf; so that through him they are delivered from condemnation, and entitled to all the benefits of his obedience: from him likewise they receive the law, as a rule enforced by his own example, and their unspeakable obligations to his redeeming love. This makes obedience pleasing, and the strength they derive from him makes it easy.

We may now proceed to inquire, in the last place, What it is to use the law lawfully? The expression implies, that it may be used unlawfully; and it is so by too many. It is not a lawful use of the law to seek justification and acceptance with God by our obedience to it; because it is not appointed for this end, or capable of answering it in our circumstances. The very attempt is a daring impeachment of the wisdom and goodness of God; for if righteousness could come by the law, then Christ has died in vain; Gal. ii. 21, iii. 21; so that such a hope is not only groundless, but sinful; and, when persisted in under the light of the Gospel, is no less than a wilful rejec-

tion of the grace of God. Again, It is an unlawful use of the
law, that is, an abuse of it, an abuse both of law and Gospel,
to pretend, that its accomplishment by Christ releases believers
from any obligation to it as a rule. Such an assertion is not
only wicked, but absurd and impossible in the highest degree:
for the law is founded in the relation between the Creator and
the creature, and must unavoidably remain in force so long as
that relation subsists. While he is God, and we are creatures,
in every possible or supposable change of state or circumstances, he must have an unrivalled claim to our reverence,
love, trust, service, and submission. No true believer can
deliberately admit a thought or a wish of being released from
his obligation of obedience to God in whole or in part; he will
rather start from it with abhorrence. But Satan labours to
drive unstable souls from one extreme to the other, and has
too often succeeded. Wearied with vain endeavours to keep
the law, that they might obtain life by it, and afterwards
taking up with a notion of the Gospel devoid of power, they
have at length despised that obedience which is the honour of a
Christian, and essentially belongs to his character, and have
abused the grace of God to licentiousness. But we have not so
learned Christ.

To speak affirmatively, The law is lawfully used as a means
of conviction of sin: for this purpose it was promulgated at
Sinai. The law entered, that sin might abound: not to make
men more wicked, though occasionally and by abuse it has
that effect, but to make them sensible how wicked they are.
Having God's law in our hands, we are no longer to form our
judgements by the maxims and customs of the world, where
evil is called good, and good evil; but are to try every principle, temper, and practice, by this standard. Could men be
prevailed upon to do this, they would soon listen to the Gospel
with attention. On some the Spirit of God does thus prevail:
then they earnestly make the jailer's inquiry, "What must I
do to be saved?" Here the work of grace begins; and the
sinner, condemned in his own conscience, is brought to Jesus
for life.

Again, When we use the law as a glass to behold the glory of
God, we use it lawfully. His glory is eminently revealed in

Christ; but much of it is with a special reference to the law, and cannot be otherwise discerned. We see the perfection and excellence of the law in his life. God was glorified by his obedience as a man. What a perfect character did he exhibit! yet it is no other than a transcript of the law. Such would have been the character of Adam and all his race, had the law been duly obeyed. It appears therefore a wise and holy institution, fully capable of displaying that perfection of conduct by which man would have answered the end of his creation. And we see the inviolable strictness of the law in his death. There the glory of God in the law is manifested. Though he was the beloved Son, and had yielded personal obedience in the utmost perfection, yet, when he stood in our place to make atonement for sin, he was not spared. From what he endured in Gethsemane and upon the cross, we learn the meaning of that awful sentence, " The soul that sinneth shall die."

Another lawful use of the law is, to consult it as a rule and pattern by which to regulate our spirit and conversation. The grace of God, received by faith, will dispose us to obedience in general, but through remaining darkness and ignorance we are much at a loss as to particulars. We are therefore sent to the law, that we may learn how to walk worthy of God, who has called us to his kingdom and glory; and every precept has its proper place and use.

Lastly, We use the law lawfully when we improve it as a test whereby to judge of the exercise of grace. Believers differ so much from what they once were, and from what many still are, that without this right use of the law, comparing themselves with their former selves, or with others, they would be prone to think more highly of their attainments than they ought. But when they recur to this standard, they sink into the dust, and adopt the language of Job, " Behold, I am vile; I cannot answer thee one of a thousand."

From hence we may collect in brief, how the law is good to them that use it lawfully. It furnishes them with a comprehensive and accurate view of the will of God, and the path of duty. By the study of the law, they acquire an habitual spiritual taste of what is right or wrong. The exercised believer,

like a skilful workman, has a rule in his hand, whereby he can
measure and determine with certainty; whereas others judge
as it were by the eye, and can only make a random guess, in
which they are generally mistaken. It likewise, by reminding
them of their deficiencies and short-comings, is a sanctified
means of making and keeping them humble; and it exceedingly
endears Jesus, the law-fulfiller, to their hearts, and puts them
in mind of their obligations to him, and of their absolute dependence upon him every moment.

If these reflections should prove acceptable to you, I have
my desire; and I send them to you by the press, in hopes that
the Lord may accompany them with his blessing to others.
The subject is of great importance, and, were it rightly understood, might conduce to settle some of the angry controversies
which have been lately agitated. Clearly to understand the
distinction, connection, and harmony between the law and the
Gospel, and their mutual subserviency to illustrate and estab-
lish each other, is a singular privilege, and a happy means of
preserving the soul from being entangled by errors on the right
hand or the left.

I am, &c.

LETTER VII

*On the Snares and Difficulties attending the Ministry of the
Gospel.*

Dear Sir,

I AM glad to hear that you are ordained, and that the Lord
is about to fix you in a place where there is a prospect of your
being greatly useful. He has given you the desire of your
heart; and I hope he has given you likewise a heart to devote
yourself, without reserve, to his service, and the service of
souls for his sake. I willingly comply with your request; and
shall, without ceremony, offer you such thoughts as occur to
me upon this occasion.

You have, doubtless, often anticipated in your mind the nature of the service to which you are now called, and made it the subject of much consideration and prayer. But a distant view of the ministry is generally very different from what it is found to be when we are actually engaged in it. The young soldier, who has never seen an enemy, may form some general notions of what is before him; but his ideas will be much more lively and diversified when he comes upon the field of battle. If the Lord was to show us the whole beforehand, who that has a due sense of his own insufficiency and weakness, would venture to engage? But he first draws us by a constraining sense of his love, and by giving us an impression of the worth of souls, and leaves us to acquire a knowledge of what is difficult and disagreeable by a gradual experience. The ministry of the Gospel, like the book which the Apostle John ate, is a bitter sweet; but the sweetness is tasted first, the bitterness is usually known afterwards, when we are so far engaged that there is no going back.

Yet I would not discourage you : it is a good and noble cause, and we serve a good and gracious Master; who, though he will make us feel our weakness and vileness, will not suffer us to sink under it. His grace is sufficient for us : and if he favours us with an humble and dependent spirit, a single eye, and a simple heart, he will make every difficulty give way, and mountains shall sink into plains before his power.

You have known something of Satan's devices while you were in private life; how he has envied your privileges, assaulted your peace, and laid snares for your feet: though the Lord would not suffer him to hurt you, he has permitted him to sift and tempt, and shoot his fiery arrows at you. Without some of this discipline, you would have been very unfit for that part of your office which consists in speaking a word in season to weary and heavy-laden souls. But you may now expect to hear from him, and to be beset by his power and subtilty in a different manner. You are now to be placed in the forefront of the battle, and to stand as it were for his mark : so far as he can prevail against you now, not yourself only, but many others, will be affected: many eyes will be upon you; and if you take a wrong step, or are ensnared into a wrong spirit, you will open the mouths of the adversaries wider, and grieve the hearts of believers more sensibly than if the same things had happened to you while you were a layman. The work of the ministry is truly honourable; but, like the post of honour in a battle, it is attended with peculiar dangers: therefore the apostle cautions Timothy, "Take heed to thyself, and to thy doctrine." To thyself in the first place, and then to thy doctrine; the latter without the former would be impracticable and vain.

You have need to be upon your guard in whatever way your first attempts to preach the Gospel may seem to operate. If you should (as may probably be the case, where the truth has been little known) meet with much opposition, you will perhaps find it a heavier trial than you are aware of; but I speak of it only as it might draw forth your corruptions, and give Satan advantage against you: and this may be two ways; first, by embittering your spirit against opposers, so as to speak in anger, to set them at defiance, or retaliate upon them in their own way; which, besides bringing guilt upon your conscience, would of course increase your difficulties, and impede your usefulness. A violent opposition against ministers and professors of the Gospel is sometimes expressed by the devil's roaring, and some people think no good can be done without it. It is allowed, that men who love darkness will show their dislike of the light; but, I believe, if the wisdom and meekness of the friends of the Gospel had been always equal to their good intentions and zeal, the devil would not have had opportunity of roaring so loud as he has sometimes done. The subject-matter of the Gospel is offence enough to the carnal heart; we must therefore expect opposition: but we should not provoke or despise it, or do anything to aggravate it. A patient continuance in well-doing, a consistency in character, and an attention to return kind offices for hard treatment, will, in a course of time, greatly soften the spirit of opposition; and instances are to be found of ministers, who are treated with some respect even by those persons in their parishes who are most averse to their doctrine. When the apostle directs us, "If it be possible, and as much as in us lies, to live peaceably with all men," he seems to intimate, that though it be difficult, it is not wholly impracticable. We cannot change the rooted prejudices of their hearts against the Gospel; but it is possible, by the Lord's blessing, to stop their mouths, and make them ashamed of discovering it, when they behold our good conversation in Christ. And it is well worth our while to cultivate this outward peace, provided we do not purchase it at the expense of truth and faithfulness; for ordinarily we cannot hope to be useful to our people, unless we give them reason to believe that we love them, and have their interest at heart. Again, opposition will hurt you, if it should give you an idea of your own importance, and lead you to dwell with a secret self-approbation upon your own faithfulness and courage in such circumstances. If you are able to stand your ground, uninfluenced either by the favour or the fear of men, you have reason to give glory to God; but remember, that you cannot thus stand an hour, unless he upholds you. It shows a wrong turn of mind, when we are very ready to speak of our trials and difficulties of this kind, and of our address and resolution in encountering them. A natural stiffness of spirit, with a desire to have self taken notice of, may make a man willing to endure those kinds of hardships, though he has but little grace in exercise: but true Christian fortitude, from a consciousness that we speak the truths of God, and are supported by his power, is a very different thing.

If you should meet with but little opposition, or if the Lord should be pleased to make your enemies your friends, you will probably be in danger from the opposite quarter. If opposition has hurt many, popularity has wounded more. To say the truth, I am in some pain for you. Your natural abilities are considerable; you have been diligent in your studies; your zeal is warm, and your spirit is lively. With these advantages, I expect to see you a popular preacher. The more you are so, the greater will your field of usefulness be: but, alas! you cannot yet know to what it will expose you. It is like walking upon ice. When you shall see an attentive congregation hanging upon your words; when you shall hear the well-meant, but often injudicious, commendations of those to whom the Lord shall make you useful; when you shall find, upon an intimation of your preaching in a strange place, people thronging from all parts to hear you, how will your heart feel? It is easy for me to advise you to be humble, and for you to acknowledge the propriety of the advice; but while human nature remains in its present state, there will be almost the same connexion between popularity and pride, as between fire and gunpowder: they cannot meet without an explosion, at least not unless the gunpowder is kept very damp. So unless the Lord is constantly moistening our hearts (if I may so speak) by the influences of his Spirit, popularity will soon set us in a blaze. You will hardly find a person who has been exposed to this fiery trial, without suffering loss. Those whom the Lord loves, he is able to keep, and he will keep them upon the whole; yet by such means, and in a course of such narrow escapes, that they shall have reason to look upon their deliverance as no less than miraculous. Sometimes, if his ministers are not watchful against the first impressions of pride, he permits it to gather strength; and then it is but a small thing that a few of their admirers may think them more than men in the pulpit, if they are left to commit such mistakes when out of it, as the weakest of the flock can discover and pity. And this will certainly be the case, while pride and self-sufficiency have the ascendant. Beware, my friend, of mistaking the ready exercise of gifts for the exercise of grace. The minister may be assisted in public for the sake of his hearers; and there is something in the nature of our public work, when surrounded by a concourse of people, that is suited to draw forth the exertion of our abilities, and to engage our attention in the outward services, when the frame of the heart may be far from being right in the sight of the Lord. When Moses smote the rock, the water followed; yet he spoke unadvisedly with his lips, and greatly displeased the Lord. However, the congregation was not disappointed for his fault, nor was he put to shame before them; but he was humbled for it afterwards. They are happy whom the Lord preserves in some degree humble, without leaving them to expose themselves to the observation of men, and to receive such wounds as are seldom healed without leaving a deep scar. But even these have much to suffer. Many distressing exercises you will probably meet with upon the best supposition, to preserve in you a due sense of your own unworthiness, and to convince you, that your ability, your acceptance, and your usefulness, depend upon a power beyond your own. Sometimes, perhaps, you will feel such an amazing difference between the frame of your spirit in public and in private, when the eyes of men are not upon you, as will make you almost ready to conclude that you are no better than an hypocrite, a mere stage-player, who derives all his pathos and exertion from the sight of the audience. At other times you will find such a total emptiness and indisposition of mind, that former seasons of liberty in preaching will appear to you like the remembrance of a dream, and you will hardly be able to persuade yourself you shall ever be capable of preaching again: the Scriptures will appear to you like a sealed book, and no text or subject afford any light or opening to determine your choice: And this perplexity may not only seize you in the study, but accompany you in the pulpit. If you are enabled at some times to speak to the people with power, and to resemble Samson, when, in the greatness of his strength, he bore away the gates of the city, you will perhaps, at others, appear before them like Samson when his locks were shorn, and he stood in fetters. So that you need not tell the people you have no sufficiency in yourself; for they will readily perceive it without your information. These things are hard to bear; yet successful popularity is not to be preserved upon easier terms: and if they are but sanctified to hide pride from you, you will have reason to number them amongst your choicest mercies.

I have but just made an entrance upon the subject of the difficulties and dangers attending the ministry. But my paper is full. If you are willing I should proceed, let me know, and I believe I can easily find enough to fill another sheet. May the Lord make you wise and watchful! That he may be the light of your eye, the strength of your arm, and the joy of your heart, is the sincere prayer of, &c.

LETTER VIII

Marks of a Call to the Ministry.

Dear Sir,

YOUR favour of the 19th February came to my hand yesterday. I have read it with attention, and very willingly sit down to offer you my thoughts. Your case reminds me of my own: my first desires towards the ministry were attended with great uncertainties and difficulties, and the perplexity of my own mind was heightened by the various and opposite judgements of my friends. The advice I have to offer is the result of painful experience and exercise, and for this reason perhaps may not be unacceptable to you. I pray our gracious Lord to make it useful.

I was long distressed, as you are, about what was or was not a proper call to the ministry; it now seems to me an easy point to solve, but perhaps will not be so to you, till the Lord shall make it clear to yourself in your own case. I have not room to say so much as I could: in brief, I think it principally includes three things:

1. A warm and earnest desire to be employed in this service. I apprehend, the man who is once moved by the Spirit of God to this work, will prefer it, if attainable, to thousands of gold and silver; so that, though he is at times intimidated by a sense of its importance and difficulty, compared with his own great insufficiency (for it is to be presumed a call of this sort, if indeed from God, will be accompanied with humility and self-abasement), yet he cannot give it up. I hold it a good rule to inquire in this point, whether the desire to preach is most fervent in our most lively and spiritual frames, and when we are most laid in the dust before the Lord? If so, it is a good sign. But if, as is sometimes the case, a person is very earnest to be a preacher to others, when he finds but little

hungerings and thirstings after grace in his own soul, it is then to be feared his zeal springs rather from a selfish principle than from the Spirit of God.

2. Besides this affectionate desire and readiness to preach, there must in due season appear some competent sufficiency as to gifts, knowledge, and utterance. Surely, if the Lord sends a man to teach others, he will furnish him with the means. I believe many have intended well in setting up for preachers, who yet went beyond or before their call in so doing. The main difference between a minister and a private Christian seems to consist in these ministerial gifts, which are imparted to him, not for his own sake, but for the edification of others. But then I say, these are to appear in due season; they are not to be expected instantaneously, but gradually, in the use of proper means. They are necessary for the discharge of the ministry; but not necessary as pre-requisites to warrant our desires after it. In your case, you are young, and have time before you; therefore I think you need not as yet perplex yourself with inquiring if you have these gifts already: it is sufficient if your desire is fixed, and you are willing, in the way of prayer and diligence, to wait upon the Lord for them: as yet you need them not.

3. That which finally evidences a proper call is a correspondent opening in Providence, by a gradual train of circumstances pointing out the means, the time, the place, of actually entering upon the work. And till this coincidence arrives, you must not expect to be always clear from hesitation in your own mind. The principal caution on this head is, not to be too hasty in catching at first appearances. If it be the Lord's will to bring you into his ministry, he has already appointed your place and service; and though you know it not at present, you shall at a proper time. If you had the talents of an angel, you could do no good with them till his hour is come, and till he leads you to the people whom he has determined to bless by your means. It is very difficult to restrain ourselves within the bounds of prudence here, when our zeal is warm, a sense of the love of Christ upon our hearts, and a tender compassion for poor sinners is ready to prompt us to break out too soon;—but he that believeth shall not make haste. I was about five years

under this constraint: sometimes I thought I must preach, though it was in the streets. I listened to everything that seemed plausible, and to many things that were not so. But the Lord graciously, and as it were insensibly, hedged up my way with thorns; otherwise, if I had been left to my own spirit, I should have put it quite out of my power to have been brought into such a sphere of usefulness, as he in his good time has been pleased to lead me to. And I can now see clearly, that at the time I would first have gone out, though my intention was, I hope, good in the main, yet I over-rated myself, and had not that spiritual judgement and experience which are requisite for so great a service. I wish you therefore to take time; and if you have a desire to enter into the Established Church, endeavour to keep your zeal within moderate bounds, and avoid everything that might unnecessarily clog your admission with difficulties. I would not have you hide your profession, or to be backward to speak for God; but avoid what looks like preaching, and be content with being a learner in the school of Christ for some years. The delay will not be lost time; you will be so much the more acquainted with the Gospel, with your own heart, and with human nature: the last is a necessary branch of a minister's knowledge, and can only be acquired by comparing what passes within us, and around us, with what we read in the word of God.

I am glad to find you have a distaste both for Arminian and Antinomian doctrines;—but let not the mistakes of others sit too heavy upon you. Be thankful for the grace that has made you to differ; be ready to give a reason of the hope that is in you with meekness and fear; but beware of engaging in disputes, without evident necessity, and some probable hope of usefulness. They tend to eat out the life and savour of religion, and to make the soul lean and dry. Where God has begun a real work of grace, incidental mistakes will be lessened by time and experience; where he has not, it is of little signification what sentiments people hold, or whether they call themselves Arminians or Calvinists.

I agree with you, it is time enough for you to think of Oxford yet; and that if your purpose is fixed, and all circumstances render it prudent and proper to devote yourself to the ministry, you will do well to spend a year or two in private studies. It would be further helpful, in this view, to place yourself where there is Gospel preaching, and a lively people. If your favourable opinion of this place should induce you to come here, I shall be very ready to give you every assistance in my power. As I have trod exactly the path you seem to be setting out in, I might so far perhaps be more serviceable than those who are in other respects much better qualified to assist you. I doubt not but in this, and every other step, you will entreat the Lord's direction; and I hope you will not forget to pray for,

Sir, your affectionate friend, &c.

LETTER IX

Advice on the Work of the Ministry.

Dear Sir,

I WOULD steal a few minutes here to write, lest I should not have leisure at home. I have not your letter with me, and therefore can only answer so far as I retain a general remembrance of the contents.

You will, doubtless, find rather perplexity than advantage from the multiplicity of advice you may receive, if you endeavour to reconcile and adopt the very different sentiments of your friends. I think it will be best to make use of them in a full latitude, that is, to correct and qualify them one by another, and to borrow a little from each, without confining yourself entirely to any. You will probably be advised to different extremes, it will then be impossible to follow both; but it may be practicable to find a middle path between them: and I believe this will generally prove the best and safest method. Only consult your own temper, and endeavour to incline rather to that side to which you are the least disposed, by the ordinary strain of your own inclination; for on that side you will be in the least danger of erring. Warm and hasty dispositions will seldom move too slow, and those who are naturally languid and cool are as little liable to over-act their part.

With respect to the particulars you instance, I have generally thought you warm and enterprising enough, and therefore thought it best to restrain you; but I meant only to hold you in, till you had acquired some further knowledge and observation both of yourself and of others. I have the pleasure to hope (especially of late) that you are become more self-diffident and wary than you were some time ago. And, therefore, as your years and time are advancing, and you have been for a tolerable space under a probation of silence, I can make no objection to your attempting sometimes to speak in select societies; but let your attempts be confined to such, I mean where you are acquainted with the people, or the leading part of them, and be upon your guard against opening yourself too much amongst strangers;—and again, I earnestly desire you would not attempt anything of this sort in a very public way, which may, perhaps, bring you under inconveniencies, and will be inconsistent with the part you ought to act (in my judgement) from the time you receive Episcopal ordination. You may remember a simile I have sometimes used of green fruit: children are impatient to have it while it is green, but persons of more judgement will wait till it is ripe. Therefore I would wish your exhortations to be brief, private, and not very frequent. Rather give yourself to reading, meditation, and prayer.

As to speaking without notes, in order to do it successfully, a fund of knowledge should be first possessed. Indeed, in such societies as I hope you will confine your attempts to, it would not be practicable to use notes; but I mean, that if you design to come out as a preacher without notes from the first, you must use double diligence in study: your reading must not be confined to the Scriptures; you should be acquainted with church-history, have a general view of divinity as a system, know something of the state of controversies in past times and at present, and indeed of the general history of mankind. I do not mean that you should enter deeply into these things; but you will need to have your mind enlarged, your ideas increased, your style and manner formed; you should read, think, write, compose, and use all diligence to exercise and strengthen your faculties. If you would speak extempore as a clergyman, you must be able to come off roundly, and to fill up your hour with various matter, in tolerable coherence, or else you will not be able to overcome the prejudice which usually prevails amongst the people. Perhaps it may be as well to use some little scheme in the note way, especially at the beginning; but a little trial will best inform you what is most expedient.

Let your backwardness to prayer and reading the Scripture be ever so great, you must strive against it. This backwardness, with the doubts you speak of, are partly from your own evil heart, but perhaps chiefly temptations of Satan : he knows, if he can keep you from drawing water out of the wells of salvation, he will have much advantage. My soul goes often mourning under the same complaints, but at times the Lord gives me a little victory. I hope he will over-rule all our trials, to make us more humble, dependent, and to give us tenderness of spirit towards the distressed. The exercised and experienced Christian, by the knowledge he has gained of his own heart, and the many difficulties he has had to struggle with, acquires a skill and compassion in dealing with others; and without such exercise, all our study, diligence, and gifts in other ways, would leave us much at a loss in some of the most important parts of our calling.

You have given yourself to the Lord for the ministry; his providence has thus far favoured your views; therefore harbour not a thought of flinching from the battle, because the enemy appears in view, but resolve to endure hardship, as a good soldier of Jesus Christ. Lift up your banner in his name; trust in him, and he will support you; but, above all things, be sure not to be either enticed or terrified from the privilege of a throne of grace.

Who your enemies are, or what they say, I know not; for I never conversed with them. Your friends here have thought you at times harsh and hasty in your manner, and rather inclining to self-confidence. These things I have often reminded you of; but I considered them as blemishes usually attendant upon youth, and which experience, temptation, and prayer, would correct. I hope and believe you will do well.

You will have a share in my prayers and best advice; and when I see occasion to offer a word of reproof, I shall not use any reserve.

Yours, &c.

LETTER X

Some Blemishes in Christian Character.

"Whatsoever things are lovely, whatsoever things are of good report . . . think on these things."—Philippians iv. 8.

Dear Sir,

THE precept which I have chosen for my motto is applicable to many particulars, which are but seldom and occasionally mentioned from the pulpit. There are improprieties of conduct, which, though usually considered as foibles that hardly deserve a severe censure, are properly sinful; for though some of them may not seem to violate any express command of Scripture, yet they are contrary to that accuracy and circumspection which become our profession. A Christian, by the tenor of his high calling, is bound to avoid even the appearance of evil; and his deportment should not only be upright as to his leading principles, but amiable and engaging, and as free as possible from every inconsistence and blemish. The characters of some valuable persons are clouded; and the influence they might otherwise have, greatly counteracted by comparatively small faults: yet faults they certainly are; and it would be well if they could be made so sensible of them, and of their ill effects, as that they might earnestly watch, and strive, and pray against them. I know not how to explain myself better than by attempting the outlines of a few portraits, to each of which I apprehend some strong resemblances may be found in real life. I do not wish to set my readers to work to find out such resemblances among their neighbours; but would advise them to examine carefully, whether they cannot, in one or other of them, discover some traces of their own features: and though I speak of men only, counterparts to the several characters may doubtless be found here and there among the women; for the imperfections and evils of a fallen nature are equally entailed upon both sexes.

AUSTERUS is a solid and exemplary Christian. He has a deep, extensive, and experimental knowledge of divine things. Inflexibly and invariably true to his principles, he stems with a noble singularity the torrent of the world, and can neither be bribed nor intimidated from the path of duty. He is a rough diamond of great intrinsic value, and would sparkle with a distinguished lustre, if he were more polished: but though the word of God is his daily study, and he prizes the precepts, as well as the promises, more than thousands of gold and silver, there is one precept he seems to have overlooked; I mean that of the apostle, BE COURTEOUS. Instead of that gentleness and condescension which will always be expected from a professed follower of the meek and lowly Jesus; there is a harshness in his manner which makes him more admired than beloved; and they who truly love him, often feel more constraint than pleasure when in his company. His intimate friends are satisfied that he is no stranger to true humility of heart; but these are few. By others he is thought proud, dogmatic, and self-important; nor can this prejudice against him be easily removed, until he can lay aside that cynical air which he has unhappily contracted.

HUMANUS is generous and benevolent. His feelings are lively, and his expressions of them strong. No one is more distant from sordid views, or less influenced by a selfish spirit. His heart burns with love to Jesus, and he is ready to receive with open arms all who love his Saviour. Yet with an upright and friendly spirit, which entitles him to the love and esteem of all who know him, he has not everything we would wish in a friend. In some respects, though not in the most criminal sense, he bridleth not his tongue. Should you, without witness or writing, intrust him with untold gold, you would run no risk of loss; but if you intrust him with a secret, you thereby put it in the possession of the public. Not that he would wilfully betray you, but it is his infirmity. He knows not how to keep a secret; it escapes from him before he is aware. So likewise as to matters of fact: in things which are of great importance, and where he is sufficiently informed, no man has a stricter regard to truth; but in the smaller concerns of common life, whether it be from credulity, or from a strange and blameable inadvertence, he frequently grieves and surprises those who know his real character, by saying *the thing that is not*. Thus they to whom he opens his very heart, dare not make him returns of equal confidence; and they who in some cases would venture their lives upon his word, in others are afraid of telling a story after him. How lamentable are such blemishes in such a person!

PRUDENS, though not of a generous natural temper, is a partaker of that grace which opens the heart, and inspires a disposition to love and to good works. He bestows not his alms to be seen of men; but they who have the best opportunities of knowing what he does for the relief of others, and of comparing it with his ability, can acquit him in good measure of the charge which another part of his conduct exposes him to. For Prudens is a great economist; and though he would not willingly wrong or injure any person, yet the meannesses to which he will submit, either to save or gain a penny in what he accounts an honest way, are a great discredit to his profession. He is punctual in fulfilling his engagements; but exceedingly hard, strict, and suspicious in making his bargains. And in his dress, and every article of his personal concerns, he is content to be so much below the station in which the providence of God has placed him, that to those who are not acquainted with his private benefactions to the poor, he appears under the hateful character of a miser, and to be governed by that love of money which the Scripture declares to be the root of all evil, and inconsistent with the true love of God and of the saints.

VOLATILIS is sufficiently exact in performing his promises in such instances as he thinks of real importance. If he bids a person depend upon his assistance, he will not disappoint his expectations. Perhaps he is equally sincere in all his promises at the time of making them; but for want of method in the management of his affairs, he is always in a hurry, always too late, and has always some engagement upon his hands with which it is impossible he can comply: yet he goes on in this

way, exposing himself and others to continual disappointments. He accepts, without a thought, proposals which are
incompatible with each other, and will perhaps undertake to
be at two or three different and distant places at the same hour.
This has been so long his practice, that nobody now expects
him till they see him. In other respects he is a good sort of
man; but this want of punctuality, which runs through his
whole deportment, puts everything out of course in which he is
concerned, abroad and at home. Volatilis excuses himself as
well as he can, and chiefly by alleging, that the things in which
he fails are of no great consequence. But he would do well to
remember, that truth is a sacred thing, and ought not to be
violated in the smallest matters, without an unforeseen and
unavoidable prevention. Such a trifling turn of spirit lessens the
weight of a person's character, though he makes no pretensions
to religion, and is a still greater blemish in a professor.

CESSATOR is not chargeable with being buried in the cares
and business of the present life to the neglect of the one thing
needful; but he greatly neglects the duties of his station. Had
he been sent into the world only to read, pray, hear sermons,
and join in religious conversation, he might pass for an eminent Christian. But though it is to be hoped, that his abounding in these exercises springs from a heart-attachment to divine
things, his conduct evidences that his judgement is weak, and
his views of his Christian calling are very narrow and defective. He does not consider, that waiting upon God in the
public and private ordinances is designed, not to excuse us
from the discharge of the duties of civil life, but to instruct,
strengthen, and qualify us for their performance. His affairs
are in disorder, and his family and connections are likely to
suffer by his indolence. He thanks God that he is not worldly-
minded; but he is an idle and unfaithful member of society,
and causes the way of truth to be evil spoken of. Of such, the
apostle has determined that, "if any man will not work, neither
should he eat."

CURIOSUS is upright and unblameable in his general deportment, and no stranger to the experience of a true Christian. His conversation upon these subjects is often satisfactory and edifying. He would be a much more agreeable com-

panion, were it not for an impertinent desire of knowing every-
body's business, and the grounds of every hint that is occasionally dropped in discourse where he is present. This puts him
upon asking a multiplicity of needless and improper questions;
and obliges those who know him, to be continually upon their
guard, and to treat him with reserve. He catechises even
strangers, and is unwilling to part with them till he is punctu-
ally informed of all their connections, employments, and
designs. For this idle curiosity he is marked and avoided as a
busy-body; and they who have the best opinion of him, cannot but wonder that a man, who appears to have so many
better things to employ his thoughts, should find leisure to
amuse himself with what does not at all concern him. Were it
not for the rules of civility, he would be affronted every day:
and if he would attend to the cold and evasive answers he
receives to his inquiries, or even to the looks with which they
are accompanied, he might learn, that, though he means no
harm, he appears to a great disadvantage, and that this prying
disposition is very unpleasing.

QUERULUS wastes much of his precious time in declaiming
against the management of public affairs; though he has
neither access to the springs which move the wheels of government, nor influence either to accelerate or retard their motions.
Our national concerns are no more affected by the remons-
trances of Querulus, than the heavenly bodies are by the disputes of astronomers. While the newspapers are the chief
sources of his intelligence, and his situation precludes him from
being a competent judge either of matters of fact, or matters of
right, why should Querulus trouble himself with politics?
This would be a weakness, if we consider him only as a member of society; but if we consider him as a Christian, it is worse
than weakness: it is a sinful conformity to the men of the
world, who look no farther than to second causes, and forget
that the LORD REIGNS. If a Christian be placed in a public
sphere of action, he should undoubtedly be faithful to his calling, and endeavour by all lawful methods to transmit our
privileges to posterity: but it would be better for Querulus to
let the dead bury the dead. There are people enough to make
a noise about political matters, who know not how to employ

their time to better purpose. Our Lord's kingdom is not of this world; and most of his people may do their country much more essential service by pleading for it in prayer, than by finding fault with things which they have no power to alter. If Querulus had opportunity of spending a few months under some of the governments upon the Continent (I may indeed say under any of them), he would probably bring home with him a more grateful sense of the Lord's goodness to him, in appointing his lot in Britain. As it is, his zeal is not only unprofitable to others, but hurtful to himself. It embitters his spirit, it diverts his thoughts from things of greater importance, and prevents him from feeling the value of those blessings, civil and religious, which he actually possesses: and could he (as he wishes) prevail on many to act in the same spirit, the governing powers might be irritated to take every opportunity of abridging that religious liberty which we are favoured with above all the nations upon earth. Let me remind Querulus, that the hour is approaching, when many things, which at present too much engross his thoughts and inflame his passions, will appear as foreign to him as what is now transacting among the Tartars or Chinese.

Other improprieties of conduct, which lessen the influence and spot the profession of some who wish well to the cause of Christ, might be enumerated, but these may suffice for a specimen.

I am, &c.

LETTER XI

Love to the Brethren.

Dear Sir,

THE apostle having said, "Marvel not, my brethren, if the world hate you," immediately subjoins, "We know that we have passed from death unto life, because we love the brethren." By the manner of his expression, he sufficiently

intimates, that the want of this love is so universal, till the
Lord plants it in the heart, that if we possess it, we may thereby be sure he has given us of his Spirit, and delivered us from
condemnation. But as the heart is deceitful, and people may
be awfully mistaken in the judgement they form of themselves,
we have need to be very sure that we rightly understand what
it is to love the brethren, before we draw the apostle's conclusion from it, and admit it as an evidence in our own favour,
that we have passed from death unto life. Let me invite you,
reader, to attend with me a little to this subject.

There are some counterfeits of this love to the brethren,
which it is to be feared have often been mistaken for it, and
have led people to think themselves something, when indeed
they were nothing. For instance:

There is a *natural* love of the brethren. People may
sincerely love their relations, friends, and benefactors, who
are of the brethren, and yet be utter strangers to the spiritual
love the apostle speaks of. So Orpah had a great affection
for Naomi, though it was not strong enough to make her willing with Ruth to leave her native country, and her idol-gods.
Natural affection can go no farther than to a personal attachment; and they who thus love the brethren, and upon no
better ground, are often disgusted with those things in them,
for which the real brethren chiefly love one another.

There is likewise a *love of convenience*. The Lord's people
are gentle, peaceful, benevolent, swift to hear, slow to speak,
slow to wrath. They are desirous of adorning the doctrine of
God their Saviour, and approving themselves followers of him
who pleased not himself, but spent his life in doing good to
others. Upon this account, they who are full of themselves,
and love to have their own way, may like their company, because they find more compliances, and less opposition from
them, than from such as themselves. For a while Laban loved
Jacob; he found him diligent and trust-worthy, and perceived
that the Lord had prospered him upon Jacob's account; but
when he saw that Jacob flourished, and apprehended he was
likely to do without him, his love was soon at an end; for it
was only founded in self-interest.

A *party-love* is also common. The objects of this are those who are of the same sentiment, worship in the same way, or are attached to the same minister. They who are united in such narrow and separate associations, may express warm affections, without giving any proof of true Christian love; for upon such grounds as these, not only professed Christians, but Jews and Turks, may be said to love one another: though it must be allowed, that believers being renewed but in part, the love which they bear to the brethren is too often debased and alloyed by a mixture of selfish affections.

The principle of true love to the brethren, is the LOVE OF GOD, that love which produceth obedience, 1 John, v. 2. " By this we know that we love the children of God, when we love God, and keep his commandments." When people are free to form their connections and friendships, the ground of their communion is in a sameness of inclination. The love spoken of is spiritual. The children of God, who therefore stand in the relation of brethren to each other, though they have too many unhappy differences in points of smaller importance, agree in the supreme love they bear to their heavenly Father, and to Jesus their Saviour; of course they agree in disliking and avoiding sin, which is contrary to the will and command of the God whom they love and worship. Upon these accounts they love one another, they are like-minded; and they live in a world where the bulk of mankind are against them, have no regard to their Beloved, and live in the sinful practices which his grace has taught them to hate. Their situation, therefore, increases their affection to each other. They are washed by the same blood, supplied by the same grace, opposed by the same enemies, and have the same heaven in view: therefore they love one another with a pure heart fervently.

The properties of this love, where its exercise is not greatly impeded by ignorance and bigotry, are such as prove its heavenly original. It extends to all who love the Lord Jesus Christ in sincerity, cannot be confined within the pale of a denomination, nor restrained to those with whom it is more immediately connected. It is gentle, and not easily provoked; hopes the best, makes allowances for infirmities, and is easily entreated. It is kind and compassionate; and this not in words only, but sympathizes with the afflicted, and relieves the indigent, according to its ability; and as it primarily respects the image of Christ in its objects, it feels a more peculiar attachment to those whom it judges to be the most spiritual, though without undervaluing or despising the weakest attainments in the true grace of the Gospel.

They are happy who thus love the brethren. They have passed from death unto life; and may plead this gracious disposition, though not before the Lord as the ground of their hope, yet against Satan, when he would tempt them to question their right to the promises. But, alas! as I before hinted, the exercise of this love, when it really is implanted, is greatly obstructed through the remaining depravity which cleaves to believers. We cannot be too watchful against those tempers which weaken the proper effects of brotherly love, and thereby have a tendency to darken the evidence of our having passed from death unto life. We live in a day when the love of many (of whom we would hope the best) is at least grown very cold. The effects of a narrow, a suspicious, a censorious, and a selfish spirit, are but too evident amongst professors of the Gospel. If I were to insist at large upon the offences of this kind which abound amongst us, I should seem almost reduced to the necessity, either of retracting what I have advanced, or of maintaining that a great part (if not the greatest part) of those who profess to know the Lord, are deceiving themselves with a form of godliness, destitute of the power: for though they may abound in knowledge and gifts, and have much to say upon the subject of Christian experience, they appear to want the great, the inimitable, the indispensable criterion of true Christianity, a love to the brethren; without which, all other seeming advantages and attainments are of no avail. How is this disagreeable dilemma to be avoided?

I believe they who are most under the influence of divine love, will join with me in lamenting their deficiency. It is well that we are not under the law, but under grace; for on whatever point we try ourselves by the standard of the sanctuary, we shall find reason to say, " Enter not into judgement with thy servant, O Lord." There is an amazing and humbling difference between the conviction we have of the beauty and excellence of divine truths, and our actual experience of their power ruling in our hearts. In our happiest hours, when we are most affected with the love of Jesus, we feel our love fervent towards his people. We wish it were always so; but we are poor inconsistent creatures, and find we can do nothing as we ought, but as we are enabled by his grace. But we trust we do not allow ourselves in what is wrong; and, notwithstanding we may in particular instances be misled by ignorance and prejudice, we do in our hearts love the brethren, account them the excellent of the earth, and desire to have our lot and portion with them in time and in eternity. We know that the love we bear them is for his sake; and when we consider his interest in *them*, and our obligations to *him*, we are ashamed and grieved that we love them no better.

If we could not conscientiously say thus much, we should have just reason to question our sincerity, and the safety of our state; for the Scriptures cannot be broken, nor can the grace of God fail of producing in some degree its proper fruits. Our Saviour, before whom we must shortly appear as our judge, has made love the characteristic of his disciples; and without some evidence that this is the prevailing disposition of our hearts, we could find little comfort in calling him God. Let not this be accounted legality, as if our dependence was upon something in ourselves. The question is not concerning the method of acceptance with God, but concerning the fruits or tokens of an accepted state. The most eminent of these, by our Lord's express declaration, is brotherly love. "By this shall all men know that you are my disciples, if you love one another." No words can be plainer; and the consequence is equally plain, however hard it may bear upon any professors, that though they could speak with the tongues of angels, had the knowledge of all mysteries, a power of working miracles, and a zeal prompting them to give their bodies to be burned in defence of the truth; yet if they love not the brethren, they are but as sounding brass or tinkling cymbals: they may make a great noise in the church and in the world; they may be wise and able men, as the words are now frequently understood; they may pray or preach with great fluency; but in the sight of God their faith is dead, and their religion is vain.

I am, &c.

LETTER XII

The Doctrines of Election and Final Perseverance.

Dear Sir,

YOUR letter breathes the spirit of a Christian, though you say
you are not a Calvinist. I should have still confined myself, in
my letters, to the great truths in which we are agreed, if you
had not invited me to touch upon the points wherein we differ.
If you were positive and peremptory in your present sentiments, I should not think it my duty to debate with you; in
that case, we might contend as much for victory as for truth.
But as you profess yourself an inquirer, and are desirous of
forming your judgement agreeably to the word of God, without
being influenced by the authority of names and parties, I willingly embrace the occasion you offer me. You say that,
though you are not prejudiced against the doctrines of election,
and perseverance of the saints, they appear to you attended
with such difficulties, that you cannot yet heartily and fully
assent to them. May the Lord, the Spirit, whose office it is to
guide his people into all truth, dictate to my pen, and accompany what I shall write with his blessing. It is not my intention to prove and illustrate these doctrines at large, or to
encounter the various objections that have been raised against
them. So much has been done in this way already, that I
could only repeat what has been said to greater advantage by
others. Nor need I refer you to the books which have been
professedly written upon this argument. In a letter to a friend,
I shall not aim at the exactness of a disputant, but only offer
a few unpremeditated hints, in the same manner as if I had
the pleasure of personally conversing with you.

Permit me to remind you, in the first place, of that important aphorism, John iii. 27 (which by the by seems to speak
strongly in favour of the doctrines in question): " A man

can receive nothing, except it be given him from heaven." If you should accede to my opinions upon my persuasion only, you would be little benefited by the exchange. The Lord alone can give us the true, vital, comfortable, and useful knowledge of his own truths. We may become wise in notions, and so far masters of a system, or scheme of doctrine, as to be able to argue, object, and fight, in favour of our own hypothesis, by dint of application, and natural abilities; but we rightly understand what we say, and whereof we affirm, no farther than we have a spiritual perception of it wrought in our hearts by the power of the Holy Ghost. It is not therefore by noisy disputation, but by humble waiting upon God in prayer, and a careful perusal of his holy word, that we are to expect a satisfactory, experimental, and efficacious knowledge of the truth as it is in Jesus. I am persuaded, that you are seeking in this way; if so, I am confident you shall not seek in vain. The Lord teaches effectually, though for the most part gradually. The path of the just is compared to the light, which is very faint at the early dawn, but shineth more and more to the perfect day.

If you sincerely seek the Lord's direction by prayer, you will of course make use of his appointed means of information, and search the Scriptures. Give me leave to offer you the following advices, while you are reading and comparing spiritual things with spiritual. First, Not to lay too great stress upon a few detached texts, but seek for that sense which is most agreeable to the general strain of the Scripture. The infallible word of God must, doubtless, be consistent with itself. If it does not appear so to us, the obscurity and seeming inconsistency must be charged to the remaining darkness and ignorance of our minds. As many locks, whose wards differ, are opened with equal ease by one master-key; so there is a certain comprehensive view of scriptural truth, which opens hard places, solves objections, and happily reconciles, illustrates, and harmonizes many texts, which to those who have not this master-key, frequently styled the *analogy of faith*, appear little less than contradictory to each other. When you obtain this key, you will be sure that you have the right sense.

Again, You will do well to consult experience as you go

along. For though this is not to be depended upon in the first
instance, but must itself be subjected to the rule of the written
word, yet it is a good subordinate help. Consider which sense
is most agreeable to what passes within you and around you,
and which best answers to the dealings of God with yourself,
and to what you can observe of his dealings with others.

Further, When you are led (as I think you will be, if you
are not already) to view the Calvinist doctrines in a favourable
light, be not afraid of embracing them, because there may be
perhaps some objections which, for want of a full possession
of the key I mentioned, you are not able to clear up; but consider if there are not as strong or stronger objections against
the other side. We are poor weak creatures; and the clearing
up of every difficulty is not what we are immediately called to,
but rather to seek that light which may strengthen and feed
our souls.

Lastly, Compare the tendency of different opinions. This is
an excellent rule, if we can fairly apply it. Whatever is from
God has a sure tendency to ascribe glory to him, to exclude
boasting from the creature, to promote the love and practice of
holiness, and increase our dependence upon his grace and
faithfulness. The Calvinists have no reason to be afraid of
resting the merits of their cause upon this issue; notwithstanding the unjust misrepresentations which have been often made
of their principles, and the ungenerous treatment of those who
would charge the miscarriage of a few individuals, as the necessary consequence of embracing those principles.

But I must check myself, or I shall finish my letter before I
properly begin my subject. You have objections to the doctrine of election. You will however agree with me, that the
Scripture does speak of it, and that in very strong and express
terms, particularly St. Paul. I have met with some sincere
people, as I believe, who have told me they could not bear to
read his 9th chapter to the Romans, but always passed it over:
so that their prejudices against election, prejudiced them
against a part of the Scripture likewise. But why so, unless
because the dreaded doctrine is maintained too plainly to be
evaded? But you will say, that some writers and preachers
attempt to put an easier sense upon the apostle's words. Let

us judge then, as I lately proposed, from experience. Admitting, what I am sure you will admit, the total depravity of human nature, how can we account for the conversion of a soul to God, unless we likewise admit an election of grace? The work must begin somewhere. Either the sinner first seeks the Lord, or the Lord first seeks the sinner. The former is impossible, if by nature we are dead in trespasses and sins; if the god of this world has blinded our eyes, and maintains the possession of our hearts; and if our carnal minds, so far from being disposed to seek God, are enmity against him. Let me appeal to yourself. I think you know yourself too well to say, that you either sought or loved the Lord first: perhaps you are conscious, that for a season, and so far as in you lay, you even resisted his call; and must have perished, if he had not made you willing in the day of his power, and saved you in defiance of yourself. In your own case, you acknowledge that he began with you; and it must be the case universally with all that are called, if the whole race of mankind are by nature enemies to God. Then further, there must be an election, unless ALL are called. But we are assured that the broad road, which is thronged with the greatest multitudes, leads to destruction. Were not you and I in this road? Were we better than those who continue in it still? What has made us differ from our former selves? *Grace.* What has made us differ from those who are now as we once were? *Grace.* Then this grace by the very terms, must be differencing, or distinguishing grace; that is, in other words, electing grace. And to suppose, that God should make this election or choice only at the time of our calling, is not only unscriptural, but contrary to the dictates of reason, and the ideas we have of the divine perfections, particularly those of omniscience and immutability. They who believe there is any power in man by nature, whereby he can turn to God, may contend for a conditional election, upon the foresight of faith and obedience: but while others dispute, let you and me admire, for we know that the Lord foresaw us (as we were) in a state utterly incapable either of believing or obeying, unless he was pleased to work in us to will and to do according to his own good pleasure.

As to final perseverance, whatever judgement we form of it

in a doctrinal view, unless we ourselves *do so persevere*, our profession of religion will be utterly vain; for only " they that endure to the end shall be saved." It should seem, that whoever believes this, and is duly apprised of his own weakness, the number and strength of his spiritual enemies, and the difficulties and dangers arising from his situation in this evil world, will at least be desirous to have (if possible) some security, that his labour and expectation shall not be in vain. To be at an uncertainty in a point of so great importance, to have nothing to trust to for our continuance in well-doing, but our own feeble efforts, our partial diligence and short-sighted care, must surely be distressing, if we rightly consider how unable we are in ourselves to withstand the forces of the world, the flesh, and the devil, which are combined against our peace. In this view, I should expect that the opposers of this doctrine, if thoroughly sensible of their state and situation, upon a supposition that they should be able to prove it unscriptural and false, would weep over their victory, and be sorry that a sentiment, so apparently suited to encourage and animate our hope, should not be founded in truth. It is not to be wondered at, that this doctrine, which gives to the Lord the glory due to his name, and provides so effectually for the comfort of his people, should be opposed and traduced by men of corrupt hearts. But it may well seem strange, that they who feel their need of it, and cannot be comfortable without it, should be afraid or unwilling to receive it. Yet many a child of light is walking in darkness upon this account. Either they are staggered by the sentiments of those whom they think wiser than themselves, or stumbled by the falls of professors who were once advocates for this doctrine, or perplexed because they cannot rightly understand those passages of Scripture which seem to speak a different language. But as light and knowledge increase, these difficulties are lessened. The Lord claims the honour, and he engages for the accomplishment of a complete salvation, that no power shall pluck his people out of his hand, or separate them from his love. Their perseverance in grace, besides being asserted in many express promises, may be proved with the fullest evidence from the unchangeableness of God, the intercession of Christ, the union which

subsists between him and his people, and from the principle of
spiritual life he has implanted in their hearts, which in its own
nature is connected with everlasting life, for grace is the seed of
glory. I have not room to enlarge on these particulars, but
refer you to the following texts, from which various strong and
invincible arguments might be drawn for their confirmation;
Luke xiv. 28-30 compared with Phil. i. 6; Heb. vii. 25 with
Rom. viii. 34-39; John xiv. 19 with John xv. 1, 2; John iv. 14.
Upon these grounds, my friend, why may not you, who have
fled for refuge to the hope set before you, and committed your
soul to Jesus, rejoice in his salvation; and say, " While Christ
is the foundation, root, head, and husband of his people, while
the word of God is Yea and Amen, while the counsels of God
are unchangeable, while we have a Mediator and High Priest
before the throne, while the Holy Spirit is willing and able to
bear witness to the truths of the Gospel, while God is wiser
than men, and stronger than Satan, so long the believer in
Jesus is and shall be safe? Heaven and earth must pass away,
but the promise, the oath, the blood, on which my soul relies,
affords me a security which can never fail."

As the doctrines of election and perseverance are comfortable, so they cut off all pretence of boasting and self-dependence, when they are truly received in the heart, and therefore tend to exalt the Saviour. Of course they stain the pride
of all human glory, and leave us nothing to glory in but the
Lord. The more we are convinced of our utter depravity and
inability from first to last, the more excellent will Jesus appear.
The *whole* may give the physician a good word, but the *sick*
alone know how to prize him. And here I cannot but remark
a difference between those who have *nothing* to trust to but free
grace, and those who ascribe a *little* at least to some good disposition and ability in man. We assent to whatever they en-
force from the word of God on the subject of sanctification.
We acknowledge its importance, its excellency, its beauty; but
we could wish they would join more with us in exalting the
Redeemer's name. Their experience seems to lead them to
talk of themselves, of the change that is wrought in them, and
the much that depends upon their own watchfulness and striving. We likewise would be thankful if we could perceive a

change wrought in us by the power of grace: we desire to be
found watching likewise. But when our hopes are most alive,
it is less from a view of the imperfect beginnings of grace in
our hearts, than from an apprehension of him who is our all
in all. His person, his love, his sufferings, his intercession,
compassion, fulness, and faithfulness,—these are our delightful
themes, which leave us little leisure, when in our best frames,
to speak of ourselves. How do our hearts soften, and our eyes
melt, when we feel some liberty in thinking and speaking of
him! For we had no help in time past, nor can have any in
time to come, but from him alone. If any persons have con-
tributed a mite to their own salvation, it was more than we
could do. If any were obedient and faithful to the first calls
and impressions of his Spirit, it was not our case. If any were
prepared to receive him beforehand, we know that we were in
a state of alienation from him. We needed sovereign irresis-
tible grace to save us, or we had been lost for ever. If there
are any who have a power of their own, we must confess ourselves poorer than they are. We cannot watch, unless he
watches with us; we cannot strive, unless he strives with us; we
cannot stand one moment, unless he holds us up; and we believe we must perish after all, unless his faithfulness is engaged
to keep us. But this we trust he will do, not for our righteousness, but for his own name's sake, and because having loved
us with an everlasting love, he has been pleased in loving kindness to draw us to himself, and to be found of us when we
sought him not.

Can you think, dear Sir, that a person who lives under the
influence of these sentiments, will desire to continue in sin
because grace abounds? No; you are too candid an observer
of men and manners, to believe the calumnies which are pro-
pagated against us. It is true, there are too many false and
empty professors amongst us; but are there none amongst those
who hold the opposite sentiments? And I would observe, that
the objection drawn from the miscarriages of reputed Calvinists
is quite beside the purpose. We maintain, that no doctrines
or means can change the heart, or produce a gracious conversation, without the efficacious power of Almighty grace; therefore, if it is found to be so in fact, it should not be charged

against our doctrine, but rather admitted as a proof and confirmation of it. We confess, that we fall sadly short in everything, and have reason to be ashamed and amazed that we are so faintly influenced by such animating principles; yet, upon the whole, our consciences bear us witness, and we hope we may declare it both to the church and to the world without just fear of contradiction, that the doctrines of grace are doctrines according to godliness.

I am, &c.

LETTER XIII

Divine Guidance.

Dear Sir,

It is well for those who are duly sensible of their own weakness and fallibility, and of the difficulties with which they are surrounded in life, that the Lord has promised to guide his people with his eye, and to cause them to hear a word behind them, saying, " This is the way, walk ye in it," when they are in danger of turning aside either to the right hand or to the left. For this purpose, he has given us the written word to be a lamp to our feet, and encouraged us to pray for the teaching of his Holy Spirit, that we may rightly understand and apply it. It is, however, too often seen, that many widely deviate from the path of duty, and commit gross and perplexing mistakes, while they profess a sincere desire to know the will of God, and think they have his warrant and authority. This must certainly be owing to misapplication of the rule by which they judge, since the rule itself is infallible, and the promise sure.   The Scripture cannot deceive us, if rightly understood; but it may, if perverted, prove the occasion of confirming us in a mistake. The Holy Spirit cannot mislead those who are under his influence; but we may suppose that we are so, when we are not. It may not be unseasonable to offer a few thoughts upon a subject of great importance to the peace of our minds, and to the honour of our holy profession.

Many have been deceived as to what they ought to do, or in forming a judgement beforehand of events in which they are nearly concerned, by expecting direction in ways which the Lord has not warranted. I shall mention some of the principal of these, for it is not easy to enumerate them all.

Some persons, when two or more things have been in view, and they could not immediately determine which to prefer, have committed their case to the Lord by prayer, and have then proceeded to cast lots: taking it for granted, that after such a solemn appeal, the turning up of the lot might be safely rested in as an answer from God. It is true, the Scripture, and indeed right reason, assures us, that the Lord disposes the lot; and there are several cases recorded in the Old Testament, in which lots were used by divine appointment; but I think neither these, nor the choosing Matthias by lot to the apostleship, are proper precedents for our conduct. In the division of the lands of Canaan, in the affair of Achan, and in the nomination of Saul to the kingdom, recourse was had to lots by God's express command. The instance of Matthias likewise was singular, such as can never happen again; namely, the choice of an apostle, who would not have been upon a par with the rest, who were chosen immediately by the Lord, unless *He* had been pleased to interpose in some extraordinary way; and all these were before the canon of Scripture was completed, and before the full descent and communication of the Holy Spirit, who was promised to dwell with the church to the end of time. Under the New-Testament dispensation, we are invited to come boldly to the throne of grace, to make our requests known to the Lord, and to cast our cares upon him: but we have neither precept nor promise respecting the use of lots; and to have recourse to them without his appointment, seems to be tempting him rather than honouring him, and to savour more of presumption than dependence. The effects likewise of this expedient have often been unhappy and hurtful: a sufficient proof how little it is to be trusted to as a guide of our conduct.

Others, when in doubt, have opened the Bible at a venture, and expected to find something to direct them in the first verse they should cast their eye upon. It is no small discredit to this practice, that the Heathens, who knew not the Bible, used some of their favourite books in the same way: and grounded their persuasions of what they ought to do, or of what should befall them, according to the passage they happened to open upon. Among the Romans, the writings of Virgil were frequently consulted upon these occasions; which gave rise to the well-known expression of the *Sortes Virgilianæ*. And indeed Virgil is as well adapted to satisfy inquirers in this way, as the Bible itself; for if people will be governed by the occurrence of a single text of Scripture, without regarding the context, or duly comparing it with the general tenor of the word of God, and with their own circumstances, they may commit the greatest extravagances, expect the greatest impossibilities, and contradict the plainest dictates of common sense, while they think they have the word of God on their side. Can the opening upon 2 Sam. vii. 3 when Nathan said unto David, "Do all that is in thine heart, for the Lord is with thee," be sufficient to determine the lawfulness or expediency of actions? Or can a glance of the eye upon our Lord's words to the woman of Canaan, Matth. xv. 28, "Be it unto thee even as thou wilt," amount to a proof, that the present earnest desire of the mind (whatever it may be) shall be surely accomplished? Yet it is certain that matters big with important consequences have been engaged in, and the most sanguine expectations formed, upon no better warrant than dipping (as it is called) upon a text of Scripture.

A sudden strong impression of a text, that seems to have some resemblance to the concern upon the mind, has been accepted by many as an infallible token that they were right, and that things would go just as they would have them; or, on the other hand, if the passage bore a threatening aspect, it has filled them with fears and disquietudes, which they have afterwards found were groundless and unnecessary. These impressions, being more out of their power than the former method, have been more generally regarded and trusted to, but have frequently proved no less delusive. It is allowed, that such impressions of a precept or a promise, as humble, animate, or comfort the soul, by giving it a lively sense of the truth contained in the words, are both profitable and pleasant; and many of the Lord's people have been instructed and supported (especially in a time of trouble) by some seasonable word of grace applied and sealed by his Spirit with power to their hearts. But if impressions or impulses are received as a voice from heaven, directing to such particular actions as could not be proved to be duties without them, a person may be unwarily misled into great evils and gross delusions; and many have been so. There is no doubt but the enemy of our souls, if permitted, can furnish us with Scriptures in abundance in this way, and for these purposes.

Some persons judge of the nature and event of their designs, by the freedom which they find in prayer. They say they commit their ways to God, seek his direction, and are favoured with much enlargement of spirit; and therefore they cannot doubt but what they have in view is acceptable in the Lord's sight. I would not absolutely reject every plea of this kind, yet without other corroborating evidence, I could not admit it in proof of what it is brought for. It is not *always* easy to determine when we have spiritual freedom in prayer. Self is deceitful; and when our hearts are much fixed and bent upon a thing, this may put words and earnestness into our mouths. Too often we first secretly determine for ourselves, and then come to ask counsel of God; in such a disposition we are ready to catch at everything that may seem to favour our darling scheme; and the Lord, for the detection and chastisement of our hypocrisy (for hypocrisy it is, though perhaps hardly perceptible to ourselves), may answer us according to our idols; see Ezek. xiv. 3, 4. Besides, the grace of prayer may be in exercise, when the subject-matter of the prayer may be founded upon a mistake, from the intervention of circumstances which we are unacquainted with. Thus I may have a friend in a distant country, I hope he is alive, I pray for him, and it is my duty so to do. The Lord, by his Spirit, assists his people in what is their present duty. If I am enabled to pray with much liberty for my distant friend, it may be a proof that the Spirit of the Lord is pleased to assist my infirmities, but it is no proof that my friend is certainly alive at the time I am praying for him: and if the next time I pray for him I should find my spirit straightened, I am not to conclude that my friend is dead, and therefore the Lord will not assist me in praying for him any longer.

Once more: A remarkable dream has sometimes been thought as decisive as any of the foregoing methods of knowing the will of God. That many wholesome and seasonable admonitions have been received in dreams, I willingly allow; but, though they may be occasionally noticed, to pay a great attention to dreams, especially to be guided by them, to form our sentiments, conduct, or expectations, upon them, is superstitious and dangerous. The promises are not made to those who dream, but to those who watch.

Upon the whole, though the Lord may give to some persons, upon some occasions, a hint or encouragement out of the common way; yet expressly to look for and seek his direction in such things as I have mentioned, is unscriptural and ensnaring. I could fill many sheets with a detail of the inconveniences and evils which have followed such a dependence, within the course of my own observation. I have seen some presuming they were doing God service, while acting in contradiction to his express commands. I have known others infatuated to believe a lie, declaring themselves assured, beyond the shadow of a doubt, of things which, after all, never came to pass; and when at length disappointed, Satan has improved the occasion to make them doubt of the plainest and most important truths, and to account their whole former experience a delusion. By these things weak believers have been stumbled, cavils and offences against the Gospel multiplied, and the ways of truth evil spoken of.

But how then may the Lord's guidance be expected? After what has been premised negatively, the question may be answered in a few words. In general, he guides and directs his people, by affording them, in answer to prayer, the light of his Holy Spirit, which enables them to understand and to love the Scriptures. The word of God is not to be used as a lottery; nor is it designed to instruct us by shreds and scraps, which, detached from their proper places, have no determinate import; but it is to furnish us with just principles, right apprehensions to regulate our judgements and affections, and thereby to influence and direct our conduct. They who study the Scriptures, in an humble dependence upon divine teaching, are convinced of their own weakness, are taught to make a true estimate of everything around them, are gradually formed into a spirit of submission to the will of God, discover the nature and duties of their several situations and relations in life, and the snares and temptations to which they are exposed. The word of God dwells richly in them, is a preservative from error, a light to their feet, and a spring of strength and consolation. By treasuring up the doctrines, precepts, promises, examples, and exhortations of Scripture, in their minds, and daily comparing themselves with the rule by which they walk, they grow into an habitual frame of spiritual wisdom, and acquire a gracious taste, which enables them to judge of right and wrong with a degree of readiness and certainty, as a musical ear judges of sounds. And they are seldom mistaken, because they are influenced by the love of Christ, which rules in their hearts, and a regard to the glory of God, which is the great object they have in view.

In particular cases, the Lord opens and shuts for them, breaks down walls of difficulty which obstruct their path, or hedges up their way with thorns, when they are in danger of going wrong, by the dispensations of his providence. They know that their concernments are in his hands; they are willing to follow whither and when he leads; but are afraid of going before him. Therefore they are not impatient: because they believe, they will not make haste, but wait daily upon him in prayer; especially when they find their hearts most engaged in any purpose or pursuit, they are most jealous of being deceived by appearances, and dare not move farther or faster than they can perceive his light shining upon their paths. I express at least their desire, if not their attainment: thus they would be. And though there are seasons when faith languishes, and self too much prevails, this is their general disposition; and the Lord, whom they serve, does not disappoint their expectations. He leads them by a right way, preserves them from a thousand snares, and satisfies them that he is and will be their guide even unto death.

I am, &c.

LETTER XIV

The Practical Influence of Faith.

Sir,

THE use and importance of faith, as it respects a sinner's justification before God, has been largely insisted on; but it is likewise of great use and importance in the daily concerns of life.
It gives evidence and subsistence to things not seen, and real-
izes the great truths of the Gospel, so as that they become
abiding and living principles of support and direction while we
are passing through this wilderness. Thus, it is as the eye
and the hand, without which we cannot take one step with
certainty, or attempt any service with success. It is to be
wished, that this practical exercise of faith were duly attended
to by all professors. We should not then meet with so many
cases that put us to a stand, and leave us at a great difficulty
to reconcile what we see in some of whom we would willingly
hope well, with what we read in Scripture of the inseparable
concomitants of a true and lively faith. For how can we but
be staggered, when we hear persons speaking the language of
assurance, that they know their acceptance with God through
Christ, and have not the least doubt of their interest in all the
promises; while at the same time we see them under the influence of unsanctified tempers, of a proud, passionate, positive, worldly, selfish, or churlish carriage?

It is not only plain, from the general tenor of Scripture, that
a covetous, a proud, or a censorious spirit, are no more consistent with the spirit of the Gospel, than drunkenness or
whoredom; but there are many express texts directly pointed
against the evils which too often are found amongst professors.
Thus the Apostle James assures us, "That if any man seemeth
to be religious, and bridleth not his tongue, his religion is
vain;" and the Apostle John, "That if any man love the

world, the love of the Father is not in him;" and he seems to apply this character to any man, whatever his profession or pretences may be, " who having this world's good, and seeing his brother have need, shutteth up his bowels of compassion from him." Surely these texts more than intimate, that the faith which justifies the soul, does likewise receive from Jesus grace for grace, whereby the heart is purified, and the conversation regulated as becomes the Gospel of Christ.

There are too many who would have the ministry of the Gospel restrained to the privileges of believers; and when the fruits of faith, and the tempers of the mind, which should be manifest in those who have " tasted that the Lord is gracious," are inculcated, think they sufficiently evade all that is said, by calling it *legal* preaching. I would be no advocate for legal preaching; but we must not be deterred, by the fear of a hard word, from declaring the whole counsel of God; and we have the authority and example of St. Paul, who was a champion of the doctrines of free grace, to animate us in exhorting professors to " walk worthy of God, who has called them to his kingdom and glory." And indeed the expression of a believer's privilege is often misunderstood. It is a believer's privilege to walk with God in the exercise of faith, and, by the power of his Spirit, to mortify the whole body of sin; to gain a growing victory over the world and self, and to make daily advances in conformity to the mind that was in Christ. And nothing that we profess to know, believe, or hope for, deserves the name of a privilege, farther than we are influenced by it to die unto sin, and to live unto righteousness. Whosoever is possessed of true faith, will not confine his inquiries to the single point of his acceptance with God, or be satisfied with the distant hope of heaven hereafter. He will be likewise solicitous how he may glorify God in the world, and enjoy such foretastes of heaven as are attainable while he is yet upon earth.

Faith, then, in its practical exercise, has for its object the whole word of God, and forms its estimate of all things with which the soul is at present concerned, according to the standard of Scripture. Like Moses, it " endures, as seeing him who is invisible." When our Lord was upon earth, and conversed with his disciples, their eyes and hearts were fixed upon him. In danger he was their defender; their guide when in perplexity; and to him they looked for the solution of all their doubts, and the supply of all their wants. He is now withdrawn from our eyes; but faith sets him still before us, for the same purposes, and, according to its degree, with the same effects, as if we actually saw him. His spiritual presence, apprehended by faith, is a restraint from evil, an encouragement to every service, and affords a present refuge and help in every time of trouble. To this is owing the delight a believer takes in ordinances, because there he meets his Lord; and to this likewise it is owing, that his religion is not confined to public occasions; but he is the same person in secret as he appears to be in the public assembly; for he worships him who sees in secret; and dares appeal to his all-seeing eye for the sincerity of his desires and intentions. By faith he is enabled to use prosperity with moderation; and knows and feels, that what the world calls good is of small value, unless it is accompanied with the presence and blessings of him whom his soul loveth. And his faith upholds him under all trials, by assuring him, that every dispensation is under the direction of his Lord; that chastisements are a token of his love; that the season, measure, and continuance of his sufferings, are appointed by infinite wisdom, and designed to work for his everlasting good; and that grace and strength shall be afforded him, according to his day. Thus, his heart being fixed, trusting in the Lord, to whom he has committed all his concerns, and knowing that his best interests are safe, he is not greatly afraid of evil tidings, but enjoys a stable peace in the midst of a changing world. For, though he cannot tell what a day may bring forth, he believes that he who has invited and enabled him to cast all his cares upon him, will suffer nothing to befall him but what shall be made subservient to his chief desires, the glory of God in the sanctification and final salvation of his soul. And if, through the weakness of his flesh, he is liable to be startled by the first impression of a sharp and sudden trial, he quickly flees to his strong refuge, remembers it is the Lord's doing, resigns himself to his will, and patiently expects a happy issue.

By the same principle of faith, a believer's conduct is regulated towards his fellow-creatures; and in the discharge of the several duties and relations of life, his great aim is to please God, and to let his light shine in the world. He believes and feels his own weakness and unworthiness, and lives upon the grace and pardoning love of his Lord. This gives him an habitual tenderness and gentleness of spirit. Humbled under a sense of much forgiveness to himself, he finds it easy to forgive others, if he has aught against any. A due sense of what he is in the sight of the Lord, preserves him from giving way to anger, positiveness, and resentment: he is not easily provoked, but is "swift to hear, slow to speak, slow to wrath;" and if offended, easy to be entreated, and disposed, not only to yield to a reconciliation, but to seek it. As Jesus is his life, and righteousness, and strength, so he is his pattern. By faith he contemplates and studies this great exemplar of philanthropy. With a holy ambition he treads in the footsteps of his Lord and Master, and learns of him to be meek and lowly, to requite injuries with kindness, and to overcome evil with good. From the same views, by faith he derives a benevolent spirit, and, according to his sphere and ability, he endeavours to promote the welfare of all around him. The law of love being thus written in his heart, and his soul set at liberty from the low and narrow dictates of a selfish spirit, his language will be truth, and his dealings equity. His promise may be depended on, without the interposition of oath, bond, or witness; and the feelings of his own heart under the direction of an enlightened conscience, and the precepts of Scripture, prompt him " to do unto others as he would desire they, in the like circumstances, should do unto him." If he is a master, he is gentle and compassionate; if a servant, he is faithful and obedient; for in either relation he acts by faith, under the eye of his Master in heaven. If he is a trader, he neither dares nor wishes to take advantage either of the ignorance or the necessities of those with whom he deals. And the same principle of love influences his whole conversation. A sense of his own infirmities makes him candid to those of others: he will not readily believe reports to their prejudice, without sufficient proof; and even then, he will not repeat them, unless he is lawfully called to it. He believes that the precept, "Speak evil of no man," is founded upon the same authority with those which forbid committing adultery or murder; and therefore he "keeps his tongue as with a bridle."

Lastly, Faith is of daily use as a preservative from a compliance with the corrupt customs and maxims of the world. The believer, though IN the world, is not OF it: by faith he triumphs over its smiles and enticements; he sees that all that is in the world, suited to gratify the desires of the flesh or the eye, is not only to be avoided as sinful, but as incompatible with his best pleasures.   He will mix with the world so far as is necessary, in the discharge of the duties of that station of life in which the providence of God has placed him, but no further. His leisure and inclinations are engaged in a different pursuit. They who fear the Lord are his chosen companions; and the blessings he derives from the word, and throne, and ordinances of grace, make him look upon the poor pleasures and amusements of those who live without God in the world with a mixture of disdain and pity; and by faith he is proof against its frowns. He will obey God rather than man; he will "have no fellowship with the unfruitful works of darkness, but will rather reprove them."   And if, upon this account, he should be despised and injuriously treated, whatever loss he suffers in such a cause, he accounts his gain, and esteems such disgrace, his glory.

I am not aiming to draw a perfect character, but to show the proper effects of that faith which justifies, which purifies the heart, worketh by love, and overcomes the world.   An habitual endeavour to possess such a frame of spirit, and thus to adorn the Gospel of Christ, and that with growing success, is what I am persuaded you are not a stranger to; and I am afraid that they who can content themselves with aiming at anything short of this in their profession, are too much strangers to themselves, and to the nature of that liberty wherewith Jesus has promised to make his people free. That you may go on from strength to strength, increasing in the light and image of our Lord and Saviour, is the sincere prayer of, &c.

LETTER XV

Family Worship.

Sir,

A NEGLECT of family-prayer is, I am afraid, too common amongst professors in this day. I am glad that you consider it both as a duty and a privilege, and are by grace determined, that when you shall commence master of a family, you will worship God with all your house. It was Abraham's commendation, that he not only served the Lord himself, but was solicitous that his children and household might serve him likewise. I trust that he who inclines your heart to walk in the footsteps of faithful Abraham, will bless you in the attempt, and give you peace in your dwelling: a mercy which is seldom enjoyed, which indeed can hardly be expected, by those families which call not upon the Lord.

Though I readily comply with your request, and should be glad if I can offer anything that may assist or animate you in your good purpose, I am afraid I shall not answer your expectations with regard to the particulars of your inquiry, concerning the most proper method of conducting family-worship. The circumstances of families are so various, that no determinate rules can be laid down, nor has the word of God prescribed any; because, being of universal obligation, it is wisely and graciously accommodated to suit the different situations of his people. You must, therefore, as to circumstantials, judge for yourself. You will do well to pursue such a method as you shall find most convenient to yourself and family, without scrupulously binding yourself, when the Scripture has left you free.

We have no positive precept enjoining us any set time for prayer, nor even how often we should pray, either in public or private; though the expressions of "continuing instant in

prayer," " praying without ceasing," and the like, plainly intimate that prayer should be frequent. Daniel prayed three
times a day; which the Psalmist speaks of as his practice likewise; and in one place declares his purpose of praising God
seven times a day. This last expression is perhaps indefinite,
not precisely seven times, but very often. Indeed a person
who lives in the exercise of faith and love, and who finds by
experience that it is good for him to draw nigh to God, will
not want to be told how often he must pray, any more than
how often he must converse with an earthly friend. Those
whom we love, we love to be much with. Love is the best
casuist, and either resolves or prevents a thousand scruples and
questions, which may perplex those who only serve God from
principles of constraint and fear. And a believer will account
those his happiest days, when he has most leisure and most
liberty of spirit for the exercise of prayer. However, I think
family-prayer cannot be said to be *stated*, unless it be performed at least daily, and, when unavoidable hindrances do
not prevent, twice a day. Though all times and seasons are
alike to the Lord, and his ear is always open whenever we have
a heart to call upon him; yet to *us* there is a peculiar suitableness in beginning and closing the day with prayer: in the morning, to acknowledge his goodness in our preservation through
the night, and entreat his presence and blessing on our persons
and callings in the course of the day; and at night to praise him
for the mercies of the day past, to humble ourselves before
him for what has been amiss, to wait on him for a renewed
manifestation of his pardoning love, and to commit ourselves
and our concerns to his care and protection while we sleep.
You will, of course, choose those hours when you are least
liable to be incommoded by the calls of business, and when the
family can assemble with the most convenience; only I would
observe, that it greatly preserves regularity and good order in
a house, to keep constantly to the same hours when it is practicable; and likewise, that it is best not to defer evening-
prayer till late, if it can be well avoided; lest some who join
in the exercise, and perhaps the person himself who leads in it,
should be too weary or sleepy to give a due attention. On
this account, I should advise to have family-prayer before

supper, where people have the choice and disposal of their own hours.

I think, with you, that it is very expedient and proper that reading a portion of the word of God should be ordinarily a part of our family-worship; so likewise to sing a hymn or psalm, or part of one, at discretion; provided there are some persons in the family who have enough of a musical ear and voice to conduct the singing in a tolerable manner; otherwise perhaps it may be better omitted. If you read and sing, as well as pray, care should be taken that the combined services do not run into an inconvenient length.

The chief thing to be attended to is, that it may be a spiritual service; and the great evil to be dreaded and guarded against in the exercise of every duty that returns frequently upon us, is formality. If a stated course of family-prayer is kept up as constantly in its season as the striking of the clock, it may come in time to be almost as mechanically performed, unless we are continually looking to the Lord to keep our hearts alive. It most frequently happens, that one or more members of a family are unconverted persons. When there are such present, a great regard should be had to them, and everything conducted with a view to their edification, that they may not be disgusted or wearied, or tempted to think that it is little more than the fashion or custom of the house; which will probably be the case, unless the master of the family is lively and earnest in performance of the duty, and likewise circumspect and consistent in every part of his behaviour at other times. By leading in the worship of God before children, servants, or strangers, a man gives bond (as it were) for his behaviour, and adds strength to every other motive which should engage him to abstain from all appearance of evil. It should be a constant check upon our language and tempers in the presence of our families, to consider that we began the day, and propose to end it with them in prayer. The apostle Peter uses this argument to influence the conduct of husbands and wives towards each other; and it is equally applicable to all the members of a family; " That your prayers be not hindered:" that is, either prevented and put off, or despoiled of all life and efficacy, by the ferment of sinful passions. On the other hand, the proper exercise of family-prayer, when recommended by a suitable deportment, is a happy means of instructing children and servants in the great truths of religion, of softening their prejudices, and inspiring them with a temper of respect and affection, which will dispose them to cheerful obedience, and make them unwilling to grieve or offend. In this instance, as in every other, we may observe, that the Lord's commands to his people are not arbitrary appointments, but that, so far as they are conscientiously complied with, they have an evident tendency and suitableness to promote our own advantage. He requires us to acknowledge him in our families, for our own sakes; not because he has need of our poor services, but because we have need of his blessing, and without the influence of his grace (which is promised to all who seek it) are sure to be unhappy in ourselves and in all our connections.

When husband and wife are happily partakers of the same faith, it seems expedient, and for their mutual good, that, besides their private devotions, and joining in family-prayer, they should pray together. They have many wants, mercies, and concerns, in common with each other, and distinct from the rest of the family. The manner in which they should improve a little time in this joint exercise cannot well be prescribed by a third person; yet I will venture to suggest one thing; and the rather, as I do not remember to have met with it in print. I conceive that it may prove much to their comfort to pray alternately, not only the husband with and for the wife, but the wife with and for the husband. The Spirit of God, by the Apostle, has expressly restrained women from the exercise of spiritual gifts in public; but I apprehend the practice I am speaking of can no way interfere with that restriction. I suppose them in private together, and then I judge it to be equally right and proper for either of them to pray with the other. Nor do I meet anything in St. Paul's writings to prevent my thinking, that if he had been a married man, he would, though an apostle, have been glad of the prayers of his wife. If you ask, how often they should pray together? I think the oftener the better, provided it does not break in upon their duties; once a day at least; and if there is a choice of hours, it might be as well at some distance from their other seasons of worship. But I would observe, as before, that in matters not expressly commanded, prudence and experience must direct.

I have written upon a supposition that you use extempore prayer; but as there are many heads of families who fear the Lord, and have not yet attained liberty to pray extempore before others, I would add, that their inability in this respect, whether real, or whether only proceeding from fear, and an undue regard to self, will not justify them in the omission of family-prayer. Helps may be procured. Mr. Jenks's Devotions are in many hands, and I doubt not but there are other excellent books of the same kind, with which I am not acquainted. If they begin with a form, not with a design to confine themselves always to one, but make it a part of their secret pleading at the throne of grace, that they may be favoured with the gift and spirit of prayer; and accustom themselves, while they use a form, to intersperse some petitions of their own; there is little doubt but they will in time find a growth in liberty and ability, and at length lay their book entirely aside. For it being every believer's duty to worship God in his family, his promise may be depended upon to give them a sufficiency in all things, for those services which he requires of them.

Happy is that family where the worship of God is constantly and conscientiously maintained. Such houses are *temples*, in which the Lord dwells, and *castles* garrisoned by a divine power. I do not say, that by honouring God in your house, you will wholly escape a share in the trials incident to the present uncertain state of things. A measure of such trials will be necessary for the exercise and manifestation of your graces, to give you a more convincing proof of the truth and sweetness of the promises made to a time of affliction, to mortify the body of sin, and to wean you more effectually from the world. But this I will confidently say, that the Lord will both honour and comfort those who thus honour him. Seasons will occur in which you shall know, and probably your neighbours shall be constrained to take notice, that he has not bid you seek him in vain. If you meet with troubles, they shall be accompanied by supports, and followed by deliverance; and you shall upon many occasions experience, that he is your protector, preserving you and yours from the evils by which you will see others suffering around you.

I have rather exceeded the limits I proposed, and therefore shall only add a request, that in your addresses at the throne of grace you will remember, &c.

LETTER XVI

Temptation.

Dear Sir,

WHAT can you expect from me on the subject of Temptation, with which you have been so much more conversant than myself? On this point I am more disposed to receive information from you, than to offer my advice. You, by the Lord's appointment, have had much business and exercise on these great waters; whereas the knowledge I have of what passes there, I have gained more from observation than from actual experience. I shall not wonder if you think I write like a novice; however, your request has the force of a command with me. I shall give you my thoughts; or rather, shall take occasion to write, not so much to you as to others, who, though they may be plunged in the depths of temptation, have not yet seen so much of the wisdom and power of God in these dispensations as yourself. I shall first inquire, Why the Lord permits some of his people to suffer such violent assaults from the powers of darkness; and then suggest a few advices to tempted souls.

The temptations of Satan (which, though not the most painful, are in reality the most dangerous) do not directly belong to my present design. I mean those, by which he is too successful in drawing many professors from the path of duty, in filling them with spiritual pride, or lulling them into carnal security. In these attempts he is often most powerful and prevalent when he is least perceived; he seldom distresses those whom he can deceive. It is chiefly when these endeavours fail, that he fights against the peace of the soul. He hates the Lord's people, grudges them all their privileges and all their comforts; and will do what he can to disquiet them, because he cannot prevail against them. And though the Lord sets such bounds to his rage as he cannot pass, and limits him both as to manner and time, he is often pleased to suffer him to discover his malice to a considerable degree; not to gratify Satan, but to humble and prove *them*; to show them what is in their hearts, to make them truly sensible of their immediate and absolute dependence upon himself, and to quicken them to watchfulness and prayer. Though temptations, in their own nature, are grievous and dreadful, yet when, by the grace of God, they are productive of these effects, they deserve to be numbered among the "all things which are appointed to work together for the good of those who love him." The light carriage, vain confidence, and woeful backslidings of many professors, might perhaps (speaking after the manner of men) have been in some measure prevented, had they been more acquainted with this spiritual warfare, and had they drunk of the cup of temptation, which but few of those who walk humbly and uprightly are exempted from tasting of, though not all in the same degree. One gracious end, therefore, that the Lord has in permitting his people to be tempted, is for the prevention of greater evils, that they may not grow proud or careless, or be ensnared by the corrupt customs of the world. In this view, I doubt not, however burdensome your trials may at some seasons prove, you are enabled, by your composed judgement, to rejoice in them, and be thankful for them. You know what you suffer now; but you know not what might have been the consequence, if you had never smarted by the fiery darts of the wicked one. You might have been taken in a more fatal snare, and been numbered with those who, by their grievous declensions and falls, have caused the ways of truth to be evil spoken of.

Another design is, for the manifestation of his power, and wisdom, and grace, in supporting the soul under such pressures as are evidently beyond its own strength to sustain. A bush on fire, and not consumed, engaged the attention of Moses. This emblem is generally applicable to the state of a Christian in the present life, but never more so than when he is in the fire of temptation. And though his heaviest sufferings of this kind are usually hidden from the notice of his fellow-creatures, yet there are other eyes always upon him. "We are," says the Apostle, "a spectacle to the world;" not only to men, but to angels also. Many things probably pass in the invisible state, in which we have a nearer concernment than we are ordinarily aware of. The beginning of the Book of Job throws some light upon this point, and informs us (of which we should have been otherwise totally ignorant) of the true cause of his uncommon sufferings. Satan had challenged him, charged him as a hypocrite, and thought he was able to prove him one, if he could have permission to attack him. The Lord, for the vindication of Job's integrity, and for the mani-festation of his own faithfulness and power in favour of his servant, was pleased to give Satan leave to try what he could do. The experiment answered many good purposes: Job was humbled, yet approved; his friends were instructed; Satan was confuted, and disappointed; and the wisdom and mercy of the Lord, in his darkest dispensations towards his people, were gloriously illustrated. This contest and the event were recorded for the direction and encouragement of his church to the end of time. Satan's malice is not abated; and though he has met with millions of disappointments, he still, like Goliath of old, defies the armies of God's Israel; he challenges the stoutest, and " desires to have them that he may sift them as wheat." Indeed he is far an overmatch for them, con-sidered as in themselves: but though they are weak, their Redeemer is mighty, and they are for ever secured by his love and intercession. " The Lord knows them that are his, and no weapon formed against them can prosper." That this may appear with the fullest evidence, Satan is allowed to assault them. We handle vessels of glass or china with caution, and endeavour to preserve them from falls and blows, because we know they are easily broken. But if a man had the art of making glass malleable, and, like iron, capable of bearing the stroke of a hammer without breaking, it is probable that, instead of locking it carefully up, he would rather, for the commendation of his skill, permit many to attempt to break it, when he knew their attempts would be in vain. Believers are compared to earthen vessels, liable in themselves to be destroyed by a small blow; but they are so strengthened and tempered by the power and supply of divine grace, that the fiercest efforts of their fiercest enemies against them may be compared to the dashing of waves against a rock. And that this may be known and noticed, they are exposed to many trials; but the united and repeated assaults of the men of the world, and the powers of darkness, afford but the more incontestible demonstration, that the Lord is with them of a truth, and that his strength is made perfect in their weakness. Surely this thought, my friend, will afford you consolation; and you will be content to suffer, if God may be glorified by you and in you.

Further, By enduring temptation, you, as a living member of the body of Christ, have the honour of being conformed to your head. He suffered, being tempted; and because he loves you, he calls you to a participation of his sufferings, and to taste of his cup; not the cup of the wrath of God; this he drank alone, and he drank it all. But in affliction he allows his people to have fellowship with him; thus they fill up the measure of his sufferings, and can say, As he was, so are we in the world. Marvel not that the world hates you, neither marvel that Satan rages against you. Should not the disciple be as his Lord? Can the servant expect or desire peace from the avowed enemies of his master? We are to follow his steps; and can we wish, if it were possible, to walk in a path strewed with flowers, when his was strewed with thorns? Let us be in nothing terrified by the power of our adversaries; which is to them an evident token of perdition, but to us of salvation, and that of God. To us it is given, not only to believe in Christ, but also to suffer for his sake. If we would make peace with the world, the world would let us alone; if we could be content to walk in the ways of sin, Satan would give us no disturbance; but because grace has rescued us from his dominion, and the love of Jesus constrains us to live to him alone, therefore the enemy, like a lion robbed of his prey, roars against us. He roars, but he cannot devour; he plots and rages, but he cannot prevail; he disquiets, but he cannot destroy. If we suffer with Christ, we shall also reign with him: in due time he will bruise Satan under our feet, make us more than conquerors, and place us where we shall hear the voice of war no more for ever.

Again, As by temptations we are conformed to the *life* of Christ, so likewise, by the sanctifying power of grace, they are made subservient to advance our conformity to his *image*; particularly as we thereby acquire a sympathy and fellow-feeling with our suffering brethren. This is eminently a branch of the mind that was in Christ. He knows how to pity and help those who are tempted, because he has been tempted himself. He knows what temptations mean, not only with that knowledge whereby he knows all things, but by experience. He well remembers what he endured in the wilderness, and in the garden; and though it is for *his* glory and *our* comfort that he suffered temptation without sin, yet for that very reason, and because he was perfectly holy, the temptations of Satan were unspeakably more bitter to him than they can be to us. The great duty and refuge of the tempted now is, to apply to him; and they have the highest encouragement to do so, in that they are assured he is touched with a feeling of our infirmities. And for the like reason they find some consolation in applying to those of their brethren who have suffered the same things. None but these can either understand or pity their complaints. If the Lord has any children who are not exercised with spiritual temptations, I am sure they are but poorly qualified to " speak a word in season to them that are weary." In this school you have acquired the tongue of the learned; and let it not seem a small thing to you, if the Lord has given you wisdom and ability, to comfort the afflicted ones: if your prayers, your conversation, and the knowledge they have of your trials, afford them some relief in a dark hour, this is an honour and a privilege which, I am persuaded, you will think you have not purchased too dear, by all that you have endured.

Once more: Temptations, by giving us a painful sensibility of the weakness of our graces, and the strength of our inward corruptions, tend to mortify the evil principles of self-dependence and self-righteousness, which are so deeply rooted in our fallen nature; to make Christ, in all his relations, offices, and characters, more precious to us; and to convince us, that without him we can do nothing. It would be easy to enlarge upon these and other advantages which the Lord enables his people to derive from the things which they suffer; so that they may say, with Samson, " Out of the eater comes forth meat;" and that what their adversary designs for their overthrow, contributes to their establishment. But I have already exceeded my limits. Enough, I hope, has been said to prove, that He has wise and gracious ends in permitting them for a season to be tossed with tempest, and not comforted. Ere long these designs will be more fully unfolded to us; and we shall be satisfied that he has done all things well. In the meanwhile it is our duty, and will be much for our comfort, to believe it upon the authority of his word.

I should now proceed to offer some advices to those who are tempted; but I am ready to say, To what purpose? When the enemy comes in like a flood; when the very foundations of hope are attacked; when suspicions are raised in the mind, not only concerning an interest in the promises, but concerning the truth of the Scripture itself; when a dark cloud blots out, not only the sense, but almost the remembrance of past comforts; when the mind is overwhelmed with torrents of blasphemous, unclean, or monstrous imaginations, things horrible and unutterable; when the fiery darts of Satan have set the corruptions of the heart in a flame; at such a season a person is little disposed or able to listen to advice. I shall, however, mention some things by which, ordinarily, Satan maintains his advantage against them in these circumstances, that they may be upon their guard as much as possible.

His principal devices are,

1. To hide from them the Lord's designs in permitting him thus to rage. Some of these I have noticed; and they should endeavour to keep them upon their minds. It is hard for them, during the violence of the storm, to conceive that any good can possibly arise from the experience of so much evil. But when the storm is over, they find that the Lord is still

mindful of them. Now, though a young soldier may well be startled at the first onset in the field of battle, it seems possible, that those who have been often engaged, should at length gain confidence from the recollection of the many instances in which they have formerly found, by the event, that the Lord was surely with them in the like difficulties, and that their fears were only groundless and imaginary. When the warfare is hottest, they have still reason to say, "Hope thou in God; for I shall yet praise him."

2. To make them utter impatient speeches, which do but aggravate their distress. It is said of Job, under his first trials, "In all this he sinned not with his lips, nor charged God foolishly." So long Satan was unable to prevail. Afterwards he opened his mouth, as Jeremiah did likewise, and cursed the day of his birth. When he once began to complain, his causes of complaint increased. We cannot prevent dreadful thoughts from arising in our hearts; but we should be cautious of giving them vent, by speaking unadvisedly. This is like letting in wind upon a smothering fire, which will make it burn more fiercely.

3. To persuade them that all they feel and tremble at arises immediately from their own hearts. Indeed it is a most awful proof of our depravity, that we feel something within ready to close with the suggestions of the enemy, in defiance of our better judgement and desires. But it is not so in all cases. It is not always easy, nor is it needful, exactly to draw the line between the temptations of Satan and our own corruptions: but sometimes it is not impossible to distinguish them. When a child of God is prompted to blaspheme the name that he adores, or to commit such evils as even unsanctified nature would recoil at, the enemy has done it, and shall be answerable for the whole guilt. The soul in this case is passive, and suffers with extreme reluctance what it more dreads than the greatest evils which can affect the body. Nor do the deepest wounds of this kind leave a scar upon the conscience, when the storm is over; which is a proof that they are not our own act.

4. To drive them from the throne of grace. Prayer, which is at all times necessary, is especially so in a time of temptation. But how hard is it to come boldly, that we may obtain

help in this time of need! but, however hard, it must be attempted. By discontinuing prayer, we give the enemy the greatest encouragement possible; for then he sees that his temptations have the effect which he intends by them, to intercept us from our stronghold. When our Lord was in an agony, he prayed the most earnestly; the ardour of his prayer increased with the distress of his soul. It would be happy if we could always imitate him in this; but too often temptations and difficulties, instead of rousing our application, dishearten and enfeeble us; so that our cries are the faintest, when we stand most in need of assistance. But so long as prayer is restrained, our burden is increased. Psalm xxxii. 3, 5. If he cannot make them omit praying, he will repeatedly endeavour to weary them by working upon the legality which cleaves so close to the heart. Satan is a hard taskmaster, when he interferes in the performance of our spiritual duties. This he does perhaps more frequently than we think of; for he can, if it serves his purpose, appear as an angel of light. When the soul is in a tempest, and attempts to pray, he will suggest, that prayer on these occasions should be protracted to such a length, and performed with such steadiness, as is found to be at that season quite impracticable. Such constrained efforts are wearisome; and, from the manner of the performance, he takes occasion to fix fresh guilt upon the conscience. Short, frequent, and fervent petitions, which will almost necessarily arise from what is felt when temptation is violent, are best suited to the case; and we need not add to the burden, by tasking ourselves beyond our power, as if we expected to be heard for our much speaking. Blessed be God that we fight with an enemy already vanquished by our Lord, and that we have a sure promise of victory. The Lord is our banner.

I am, &c.

LETTER XVII

Controversy.

Dear Sir,

As you are likely to be engaged in controversy, and your
love of truth is joined with a natural warmth of temper, my
friendship makes me solicitous on your behalf. You are of
the strongest side; for truth is great, and must prevail; so that
a person of abilities inferior to yours, might take the field with
a confidence of victory. I am not therefore anxious for the
event of the battle; but I would have you more than a con-
queror, and to triumph not only over your adversary, but over
yourself. If you cannot be vanquished, you may be wounded.
To preserve you from such wounds as might give you cause
of weeping over your conquests, I would present you with
some considerations, which, if duly attended to, will do you
the service of a coat of mail; such armour, that you need not
complain, as David did of Saul's, that it will be more cumber-
some than useful; for you will easily perceive it is taken from
that great magazine provided for the Christian soldier, the
word of God. I take it for granted, that you will not expect
any apology for my freedom, and therefore I shall not offer
one. For method's sake, I may reduce my advice to three
heads, respecting your opponent, the public, and yourself.

As to your opponent, I wish, that before you set pen to
paper against him, and during the whole time you are preparing your answer, you may commend him by earnest prayer
to the Lord's teaching and blessing. This practice will have a
direct tendency to conciliate your heart to love and pity him;
and such a disposition will have a good influence upon every
page you write. If you account him a believer, though greatly
mistaken in the subject of debate between you, the words of
David to Joab, concerning Absalom, are very applicable:
"Deal gently with him for my sake." The Lord loves him

and bears with him; therefore you must not despise him, or treat him harshly. The Lord bears with you likewise, and expects that you should show tenderness to others, from a sense of the much forgiveness you need yourself. In a little while you will meet in heaven; he will then be dearer to you than the nearest friend you have upon earth is to you now. Anticipate that period in your thoughts; and though you may find it necessary to oppose his errors, view him personally as a kindred soul, with whom you are to be happy in Christ for ever. But if you look upon him as an unconverted person, in a state of enmity against God and his grace (a supposition which, without good evidence, you should be very unwilling to admit), he is a more proper object of your compassion than of your anger. Alas! " he knows not what he does." But you know who has made you to differ. If God, in his sovereign pleasure, had so appointed, you might have been as he is now; and he, instead of you, might have been set for the defence of the Gospel. You were both equally blind by nature. If you attend to this, you will not reproach or hate him, because the Lord has been pleased to open your eyes, and not his. Of all people who engage in controversy, we, who are called Cal- vinists, are most expressly bound by our own principles to the exercise of gentleness and moderation. If, indeed, they who differ from us have a power of changing themselves, if they can open their own eyes, and soften their own hearts, then we might with less inconsistency be offended at their obstinacy; but if we believe the very contrary to this, our part is, not to strive, but in meekness to instruct those who oppose, " if per- adventure God will give them repentance to the acknow- ledgement of the truth." If you write with a desire of being an instrument of correcting mistakes, you will of course be cautious of laying stumbling-blocks in the way of the blind, or of using any expressions that may exasperate their passions, confirm them in their prejudices, and thereby make their con- viction, humanly speaking, more impracticable.

By printing, you will appeal to the public; where your readers may be ranged under three divisions. First, such as differ from you in principle. Concerning these I may refer you to what I have already said. Though you have your eye upon one person chiefly, there are many like-minded with him; and the same reasoning will hold, whether as to one or to a million. There will be likewise many who pay too little regard to religion to have any settled system of their own, and yet are pre-engaged in favour of those sentiments which are least repugnant to the good opinion men naturally have of themselves. These are very incompetent judges of doctrines; but they can form a tolerable judgement of a writer's spirit. They know that meekness, humility, and love, are the characteristics of a Christian temper; and though they affect to treat the doctrines of grace as mere notions and speculations, which, supposing they adopted them, would have no salutary influence upon their conduct; yet from us, who profess these principles, they always expect such dispositions as correspond with the precepts of the Gospel. They are quick-sighted to discern when we deviate from such a spirit, and avail themselves of it to justify their contempt of our arguments. The Scriptural maxim, that "the wrath of man worketh not the righteousness of God," is verified by daily observation. If our zeal is embittered by expressions of anger, invective, or scorn, we may think we are doing service to the cause of truth, when in reality we shall only bring it into discredit. The weapons of our warfare, and which alone are powerful to break down the strongholds of error, are not carnal but spiritual; arguments fairly drawn from Scripture and experience, and enforced by such a mild address as may persuade our readers, that, whether we can convince them or not, we wish well to their souls, and contend only for the truth's sake; if we can satisfy them that we act upon these motives, our point is half gained; they will be more disposed to consider calmly what we offer; and if they should still dissent from our opinions, they will be constrained to approve our intentions.

You will have a third class of readers, who being of your own sentiments, will readily approve of what you advance, and may be further established and confirmed in their views of the Scripture doctrines, by a clear and masterly elucidation of your subject. You may be instrumental to their edification, if the law of kindness as well as of truth regulates your pen, otherwise you may do them harm There is a principle of self, which disposes us to despise those who differ from us; and we are often under its influence, when we think we are only showing a becoming zeal in the cause of God. I readily believe, that the leading points of Arminianism spring from, and are nourished by, the pride of the human heart; but I should be glad if the reverse was always true; and that to embrace what are called the Calvinistic doctrines was an infallible token of a humble mind. I think I have known some Arminians, that is, persons who, for want of clearer light, have been afraid of receiving the doctrines of free grace, who yet have given evidence that their hearts were in a degree humbled before the Lord. And I am afraid there are Calvinists, who, while they account it a proof of their humility, that they are willing in words to abase the creature, and to give all the glory of salvation to the Lord, yet know not what manner of spirit they are of. Whatever it be that makes us trust in ourselves that we are comparatively wise or good, so as to treat those with contempt who do not subscribe to our doctrines, or follow our party, is a proof and fruit of a self-righteous spirit. Self-righteousness can feed upon doctrines, as well as upon works; and a man may have the heart of a Pharisee, while his head is stored with orthodox notions of the unworthiness of the creature, and the riches of free grace. Yea, I would add, the best of men are not wholly free from this leaven; and therefore are too apt to be pleased with such representations as hold up our adversaries to ridicule, and by consequence flatter our own superior judgements. Controversies for the most part, are so managed as to indulge rather than to repress this wrong disposition; and therefore, generally speaking, they are productive of little good. They provoke those whom they should convince, and puff up those whom they should edify. I hope your performance will savour of a spirit of true humility, and be a means of promoting it in others.

This leads me, in the last place, to consider your own concern in your present undertaking. It seems a laudable service to defend the faith once delivered to the saints; we are commanded to contend earnestly for it, and to convince gainsayers. If ever such defences were seasonable and expedient, they appear to be so in our day, when errors abound on all sides, and every truth of the Gospel is either directly denied, or grossly misrepresented. And yet we find but very few writers of controversy who have not been manifestly hurt by it. Either they grow in a sense of their own importance, or imbibe an angry contentious spirit, or they insensibly withdraw their attention from those things which are the food and immediate support of the life of faith, and spend their time and strength upon matters which at most are but of a secondary value. This shows, that if the service is honourable, it is dangerous. What will it profit a man if he gains his cause, and silences his adversary, if at the same time he loses that humble tender frame of spirit in which the Lord delights, and to which the promise of his presence is made? Your aim, I doubt not, is good; but you have need to watch and pray, for you will find Satan at your right hand to resist you: he will try to debase your views; and though you set out in defence of the cause of God, if you are not continually looking to the Lord to keep you, it may become your own cause, and awaken in you those tempers which are inconsistent with true peace of mind, and will surely obstruct communion with God. Be upon your guard against admitting anything personal into the debate. If you think you have been ill treated, you will have an opportunity of showing that you are a disciple of Jesus, who, "when he was reviled, reviled not again; when he suffered, he threatened not." This is our pattern, thus we are to speak and write for God, "not rendering railing for railing, but contrariwise blessing; knowing that hereunto we are called." The wisdom that is from above is not only pure, but peaceable and gentle; and the want of these qualifications, like the dead fly in the pot of ointment, will spoil the savour and efficacy of our labours. If we act in a wrong spirit, we shall bring little glory to God, do little good to our fellow-creatures, and procure neither honour nor comfort to ourselves. If you can be content with showing your wit, and gaining the laugh on your side, you have an easy task; but I hope you have a far nobler aim, and that, sensible of the solemn importance of Gospel-truths, and the compassion due to the souls of men, you would rather be a means of removing prejudices in a single instance, than obtain the empty applause of thousands. Go forth, therefore, in the name and strength of the Lord of Hosts, speaking the truth in love; and may he give you a witness in many hearts, that you are taught of God, and favoured with the unction of his Holy Spirit.

I am, &c.

LETTER XVIII

Man in his Fallen Estate (1)

Dear Sir,

WE hear much in the present day of the dignity of human nature. And it is allowed that man was an excellent creature as he came out of the hands of God; but if we consider this question with a view to fallen man, as depraved by sin, how can we but join with the Psalmist in wonder that the great God should make any account of him?

Fallen as man is from his original state of happiness and holiness, his natural faculties and abilities afford sufficient evidence that the hand which made him is divine. He is capable of great things. His understanding, will, affections, imagination, and memory, are noble and amazing powers. But view him in a moral light, as an intelligent being, incessantly dependent upon God, accountable to him, and appointed by him to a state of existence in an unchangeable world; considered in this relation, man is a monster, a vile, base, stupid, obstinate and mischievous creature; no words can fully describe him. Man, with all his boasted understanding and attainments, is a fool: so long as he is destitute of the saving grace of God, his conduct, as to his most important concernments, is more absurd and inconsistent than that of the meanest idiot; with respect to his affections and pursuits, he is degraded far below the beasts; and for the malignity and wickedness of his will, can be compared to nothing so properly as to the devil.

The question here is not concerning this or that man, a Nero or a Heliogabalus, but concerning human nature, the whole race of mankind, the few excepted who are born of God. There is indeed a difference amongst men, but it is owing to the restraints of Divine Providence, without which earth would be the very image of hell. A wolf or a lion, while chained, cannot do so much mischief as if they were loose, but the nature is the same in the whole species. Education and interest, fear and shame, human laws, and the secret power of God over the mind, combine to form many characters that are externally decent and respectable; and even the most abandoned are under a restraint which prevents them from manifesting a thousandth part of the wickedness which is in their hearts. But the heart itself is universally deceitful, and desperately wicked.

Man is a fool. He can indeed measure the earth, and almost count the stars; he abounds in arts and inventions, in science and policy,—and shall he then be called a fool? The ancient Heathens, the inhabitants of Egypt, Greece, and Rome, were eminent for this kind of wisdom. They are to this day studied as models by those who aim to excel in history, poetry, painting, architecture, and other exertions of human genius, which are suited to polish the manners without improving the heart. But their most admired philosophers, legislators, logicians, orators, and artists, were as destitute as infants or idiots of that knowledge which alone deserves the name of true wisdom. Professing themselves to be wise, they became fools. Ignorant and regardless of God, yet conscious of their weakness, and of their dependence upon a power above their own, and stimulated by an inward principle of fear, of which they knew neither the origin nor right application, they worshipped the creature instead of the Creator, yea, placed their trust in stocks and stones, in the works of men's hands, in non-entities and chimeras. An acquaintance with their mythology, or system of religious fables, passes with us for a considerable branch of learning, because it is drawn from ancient books written in languages not known to the vulgar; but in point of certainty or truth, we might receive as much satisfaction from a collection of dreams, or from the ravings of lunatics. If, therefore, we admit these admired sages as a tolerable specimen of mankind, must we not confess that man in his best estate, while uninstructed by the Spirit of God, is a fool? But are we wiser than they? Not in the least, till the grace of God makes us so. Our superior advantages only show our folly in a more striking light. Why do we account any persons foolish? A fool has no sound judgement; he is governed wholly by appearances, and would prefer a fine coat to the writings of a large estate. He pays no regard to consequences. Fools have sometimes hurt or killed their best friends, and thought they did no harm. A fool cannot reason, therefore arguments are lost upon him. At one time, if tied with a straw, he dares not stir; at another time, perhaps, he can hardly be persuaded to move, though the house were on fire. Are these the characteristics of a fool? Then there is no fool like the sinner, who prefers the toys of earth to the happiness of heaven; who is held in bondage by the foolish customs of the world, and is more afraid of the breath of man, than of the wrath of God.

Again, Man in his natural state is a beast, yea below the beasts that perish. In two things he strongly resembles them; in looking no higher than to sensual gratifications, and in that selfishness of spirit which prompts him to propose himself and his own interest as his proper and highest end. But in many respects he sinks sadly beneath them. Unnatural lusts, and the want of natural affection toward their offspring, are abominations not to be found among the brute creation. What shall we say of mothers destroying their children with their own hands, or of the horrid act of self-murder! Men are worse than beasts likewise in their obstinacy; they will not be warned. If a beast escapes from a trap, he will be cautious how he goes near it again, and in vain is the net spread in the sight of any bird. But man, though he be often reproved, hardens his neck; he rushes upon his ruin with his eyes open, and can defy God to his face, and dare damnation.

Once more, Let us observe how man resembles the devil. There are spiritual sins, and from these in their height the Scripture teaches us to judge of Satan's character. Every feature in this description is strong in man; so that what our Lord said to the Jews is of general application, "Ye are of your father the devil, and the lusts of your father you will do." Man resembles Satan in *pride*; this stupid, wicked creature values himself upon his wisdom, power, and virtue, and will talk of being saved by his good works; though if *he* can, Satan himself need not despair. He resembles him in *malice*; and this diabolical disposition often proceeds to murder, and would daily if the Lord did not restrain it. He derives from Satan the hateful spirit of *envy*: he is often tormented beyond expression, by beholding the prosperity of his neighbours; and proportionably pleased with their calamities, though he gains no other advantage from them than the gratification of this rancorous principle. He bears the image likewise of Satan in his *cruelty*. This evil is bound up in the heart even of a child. A disposition to take pleasure in giving pain to others appears very early. Children, if left to themselves, soon feel a gratification in torturing insects and animals. What misery does the wanton cruelty of men inflict upon cocks, dogs, bulls, bears, and other creatures, which they seem to think were formed for no other end than to feast their savage spirits with their torments! If we form our judgement of men, when they seem most pleased, and have neither anger nor resentment to plead in their excuse, it is too evident, even from the nature of their amusements, whose they are and whom they serve; and they are the worst of enemies to each other. Think of the horrors of war, the rage of duellists, of the murders and assassinations with which the world is filled, and then say, " Lord, what is man!" Further, if *deceit* and *treachery* belong to Satan's character, then surely man resembles him. Is not the universal observation, and complaint of all ages, an affecting comment upon the prophet's words, " Trust ye not in a friend, put not confidence in a guide, keep the doors of thy mouth from her that lieth in thy bosom, for they hunt every man his brother with a net." How many have at this moment cause to say with David, " The words of his mouth were smoother than butter, but war was in his heart; his words were softer than oil, yet were they drawn swords." Again, like Satan, men are eager in tempting others to sin; not content to damn themselves, they employ all their arts and influence to draw as many as they can with them into the same destruction. Lastly, In direct opposition to God and goodness, in contemptuous enmity to the Gospel of his grace, and a bitter persecuting spirit against those who profess it, Satan himself can hardly exceed them. Herein, indeed, they are his agents and willing servants; and because the blessed God is himself out of their reach, they labour to show their despite to him in the persons of his people.

I have drawn but a sketch, a few outlines of the picture of fallen man. To give an exact copy of him, to charge every feature with its full aggravation of horror, and to paint him *as he is*, would be impossible. Enough has been observed to illustrate the propriety of the exclamation, "Lord, what is man!" Perhaps some of my readers may attempt to deny or extenuate the charge, and may plead that I have not been describing mankind, but some of the most abandoned of the species, who hardly deserve the name of men. But I have already provided against this exception. It is human nature I describe; and the vilest and most profligate individuals cannot sin beyond the powers and limits of that nature which they possess in common with the more mild and moderate. Though there may be a difference in the fruitfulness of trees, yet the production of one apple decides the nature of the tree upon which it grew, as certainly as if it had produced a thousand: so in the present case, should it be allowed that these enormities cannot be found in *all persons*, it would be a sufficient confirmation of what I have advanced, if they can be found in *any*; unless it could be likewise proved, that those who appeared more wicked than others, were of a different species from the rest. But I need not make this concession; they must be insensible indeed who do not feel something within them so very contrary to our common notions of goodness, as would perhaps make them rather submit to be banished from human society, than to be compelled *bona fide* to disclose to their fellow-creatures every thought and desire which arises in their hearts.

Many useful reflections may be drawn from this unpleasing subject. We cannot at present conceive how much we owe to the guardian care of Divine Providence, that any of us are preserved in peace and safety for a single day in such a world as this. Live where we will, we have those near us, who, both by nature, and by the power which Satan has over them, are capable of the most atrocious crimes. But he whom they know not, restrains them so that they cannot do the things that they would. When he suspends the restraint, they act immediately; then we hear of murders, rapes, and outrages. But did not the Lord reign with a strong hand, such evils would be perpetrated every hour, and no one would be safe in the house or in the field. His ordinance of civil government is one great means of preserving the peace of society; but this is in many cases inadequate. The heart of man, when fully bent upon evil, will not be intimidated or stopped by gibbets and racks.

How wonderful is the love of God in giving his Son to die for such wretches! And how strong and absolute is the necessity of a new birth, if we would be happy! Can beasts and devils inherit the kingdom of God? The due consideration of this subject is likewise needful, to preserve believers in an humble, thankful, watchful frame of spirit. Such we once were, and such, with respect to the natural principle remaining in us, which the apostle calls the flesh or the old man, we still are. The propensities of fallen nature are not eradicated in the children of God, though by grace they are made partakers of a new principle, which enables them, in the Lord's strength, to resist and mortify the body of sin, so that it cannot reign in them. Yet they are liable to sad surprisals; and the histories of Aaron, David, Solomon, and Peter, are left on record, to teach us what evil is latent in the hearts of the best men, and what they are capable of doing if left but a little to themselves. "Lord, what is man!"

I am, &c.

LETTER XIX

Man in his Fallen Estate (2).

Dear Sir,

THE nature of fallen man agrees to the description the apostle has given us of his boasted wisdom: it is earthly, sensual, devilish. I have attempted some general delineation of it in the preceding letter; but the height of its malignity cannot be properly estimated, unless we consider its actings with respect to the light of the Gospel. The Jews were extremely wicked at the time of our Lord's appearance upon earth; yet he said of them, " If I had not come and spoken to them, they had not had sin;" that is, as the light and power of his ministry deprived them of all excuse for continuing in sin, so it proved the occasion of showing their wickedness in the most aggravated manner; and all their other sins were but faint proofs of the true state of their hearts, if compared with the discovery they made of themselves, by their pertinacious opposition to *him*. In this sense, what the apostle has observed of the law of Moses, may be applied to the Gospel of Christ: it entered, that sin might abound. If we would estimate the utmost exertions of human depravity, and the strongest effects it is capable of producing, we must select our instances from the conduct of those to whom the Gospel is known. The Indians, who roast their enemies alive, give sufficient proof that man is *barbarous to his own kind*; which may likewise be easily demonstrated without going so far from home; but the preaching of the Gospel discovers *the enmity of the heart against God*, in ways and degrees of which unenlightened savages and heathens are not capable.

By the Gospel, I now mean not merely the doctrine of salvation as it lies in the holy Scripture, but that public and authoritative dispensation of this doctrine, which the Lord Jesus Christ has committed to his true ministers; who having been themselves, by the power of his grace, brought out of darkness into marvellous light, are by his Holy Spirit qualified and sent forth to declare to their fellow-sinners what they have seen, and felt, and tasted, of the word of life. Their commission is, to exalt the Lord alone, to stain the pride of all human glory. They are to set forth the evil and demerit of sin, the strictness, spirituality, and sanction of the law of God, the total apostasy of mankind; and from these premises to demonstrate the utter impossibility of a sinner's escaping condemnation by any works or endeavours of his own; and then to proclaim a full and free salvation from sin and wrath, by faith in the name, blood, obedience, and mediation of God manifest in the flesh; together with a denunciation of eternal misery to all who shall finally reject the testimony which God has given of his Son. Though these several branches of the will of God respecting sinners, and other truths in connection with them, are plainly revealed and repeatedly inculcated in the Bible; and though the Bible is to be found in almost every house, yet we see, in fact, it is a sealed book, little read, little understood, and therefore but little regarded, except in those places which the Lord is pleased to favour with ministers who can confirm them from their own experience, and who, by a sense of his constraining love, and the worth of souls, are animated to make the faithful discharge of their ministry the one great business of their lives: who aim not to possess the wealth, but to promote the welfare of their hearers; are equally regardless of the frowns or smiles of the world; and count not their lives dear, so that they may be wise and successful in winning souls to Christ.

When the Gospel, in this sense of the word, first comes to a place, though the people are going on in sin, they may be said to sin ignorantly; they have not yet been warned of their danger. Some are drinking down iniquity like water; others more soberly burying themselves alive in the cares and business of the world; others find a little time for what they call religious duties, which they persevere in, though they are utter strangers to the nature or the pleasure of spiritual worship; partly, as thereby they think to bargain with God and to make amends for such sins as they do not choose to relinquish; and partly because it gratifies their pride, and affords them (as they think) some ground for saying, "God, I thank thee I am not as other men." The preached Gospel declares the vanity and danger of these several ways which sinners choose to walk in. It declares, and demonstrates, that, different as they appear from each other, they are equally remote from the path of safety and peace, and all tend to the same point, the destruction of those who persist in them. At the same time it provides against that despair into which men would be otherwise plunged, when convinced of their sins, by revealing the immense love of God, the glory and grace of Christ, and inviting all to come to him, that they may obtain pardon, life, and happiness. In a word, it shows the pit of hell under men's feet, and opens the gate and points out the way to heaven. Let us now briefly observe the effects it produces in those who do not receive it as the power of God unto salvation. These effects are various, as tempers and circumstances vary; but they may all lead us to adopt the Psalmist's exclamation, "Lord, what is man!"

Many who have heard the Gospel once or a few times, will hear it no more; it awakens their scorn, their hatred and rage. They pour contempt upon the wisdom of God, despise his goodness, defy his power; and their very looks express the spirit of the rebellious Jews, who told the prophet Jeremiah to his face, "As to the word which thou hast spoken to us in the name of the Lord, we will not hearken to thee at all." The ministers who preach it, are accounted men that turn the world upside down; and the people who receive it, fools or hypocrites. The word of the Lord is a burden to them, and they hate it with a perfect hatred. How strongly is the disposition of the natural heart manifested, by the confusion which often takes place in families, where the Lord is pleased to awaken one or two in a house, while the rest remain in their sins! To profess, or even to be suspected of, an attachment to the Gospel of Christ, is frequently considered and treated as the worst of crimes, sufficient to cancel the strongest obligations of relation or friendship. Parents, upon such a provocation, will hate their children, and children ridicule their parents: many find, agreeable to our Lord's declaration, that from the time a sense of his love engaged their hearts to love him again, their worst foes have been those of their own household; and that they who expressed the greatest love and tenderness for them before their conversion, can now hardly bear to see them.

The bulk of a people will perhaps continue to hear, at least now and then; and to those who do, the Spirit of God usually, at one time or other, bears testimony to the truth: their consciences are struck, and for a season they believe and tremble. But what is the consequence? No man who has taken poison seeks more earnestly or speedily for an antidote, than those do for something to stifle and smother their convictions. They

run to company, to drink, to anything, for relief against the
unwelcome intrusion of serious thoughts; and when they succeed, and recover their former indifference, they rejoice as if
they had escaped some great danger. The next step is, to
ridicule their own convictions; and next to that, if they see any
of their acquaintance under the like impressions, to use every
art, and strain every nerve, that they may render them as
obstinate as themselves. For this purpose, they watch as a
fowler for the bird, flatter or revile, tempt or threaten; and if
they can prevail, and are the occasion of hardening any in
their sins, they rejoice and triumph as if they accounted it
their interest and their glory to ruin the souls of their fellow-
creatures.

By frequent hearing, they receive more light. They are
compelled to know, whether they will or not, that the wrath
of God hangs over the children of disobedience. They carry
a sting in their consciences, and at times feel themselves most
miserable, and cannot but wish they had never been born, or
that they had been dogs or toads, rather than rational creatures. Yet they harden themselves still more. They affect
to be happy and at ease and force themselves to wear a smile
when anguish preys upon their hearts. They blaspheme the
way of truth, watch for the faults of professors, and with a
malicious joy publish and aggravate them. They see perhaps
how the wicked die, but are not alarmed; they see the righteous
die, but are not moved. Neither providences nor ordinances,
mercies nor judgements, can stop them, for they are determined to go on and perish with their eyes open, rather than
submit to the Gospel.

But they do not always openly reject the Gospel-truths.
Some who profess to approve and receive them, do thereby discover the evils of the heart of man, if possible, in a yet stronger
light. They make Christ the minister of sin, and turn his grace
into licentiousness. Like Judas, they say, Hail, Master! and
betray him. This is the highest pitch of iniquity. They per-
vert all the doctrines of the Gospel. From election they draw
an excuse for continuing in their evil ways; and contend for
salvation without works, because they love not obedience.
They extol the righteousness of Christ, but hold it in opposi-

tion to personal holiness. In a word, because they hear that God is good, they determine to persist in evil. "Lord, what is man!"

Thus wilful and impenitent sinners go on from bad to worse, deceiving and being deceived. The word which they despise becomes to them a savour of death unto death. They take different courses, but all are travelling down to the pit; and, unless sovereign mercy interpose, will soon sink to rise no more. The final event is usually twofold. Many, after they have been more or less shaken by the word, settle in formality. If hearing would supply the place of faith, love, and obedience, they would do well; but by degrees they become sermon-proof: the truths which once struck them lose their power by being often heard; and thus multitudes live and die in darkness, though the light has long shone around them. Others are more openly given up to a reprobate mind. Contempt of the Gospel makes Infidels, Deists, and Atheists. They are filled with a spirit of delusion to believe a lie. These are scoffers, walking after their own lusts; for where the principles of religion are given up, the conduct will be vile and abominable. Such persons sport themselves with their own deceivings, and strongly prove the truth of the Gospel while they dispute against it. We often find that people of this cast have formerly been the subjects of strong convictions; but when the evil spirit has seemed to depart for a season, and returns again, the last state of that person is worse than the first.

It is not improbable that some of my readers may meet with their own characters under one or other of the views I have given of the desperate wickedness of the heart, in its actings against the truth. May the Spirit of God constrain them to read with attention! Your case is dangerous, but I would hope not utterly desperate. Jesus is mighty to save. His grace can pardon the most aggravated offences, and subdue the most inveterate habits of sin. The Gospel you have hitherto slighted, resisted, or opposed, is still the power of God unto salvation. The blood of Jesus, upon which you have hitherto trampled, speaks better things than the blood of Abel, and is of virtue to cleanse those whose sins are scarlet and crimson, and to make them white as snow. As yet you are spared; but it is high time to stop, to throw down your arms of rebellion, and humble yourselves at his feet. If you do, you may yet escape; but if not, know assuredly that wrath is coming upon you to the uttermost; and you will shortly find, to your unspeakable dismay, that it is a fearful thing to fall into the hands of the living God.

I am, &c.

LETTER XX

Causes, Nature, and Marks of a Decline in Grace.

My Lord,

I REMEMBER, when I once had the pleasure of waiting on you, you were pleased to begin an interesting conversation, which, to my concern, was interrupted. The subject was concerning the causes, nature, and marks of a decline in grace; how it happens that we lose that warm impression of divine things, which in some favoured moments we think it almost impossible to forget; how far this change of frame is consistent with a spiritual growth in other respects; how to form a comparative judgement of our proficiency upon the whole; and by what steps the losses we sustain from our necessary connexion with a sinful nature and a sinful world may be retrieved from time to time. I beg your Lordship's permission to fill up the paper with a view to these inquiries. I do not mean to offer a laboured essay on them, but such thoughts as shall occur while the pen is in my hand.

The awakened soul (especially when, after a season of distress and terror, it begins to taste that the Lord is gracious), finds itself as in a new world. No change in outward life can be so sensible, so affecting. No wonder, then, that at such a time little else can be thought of;—the transition from darkness to light, from a sense of wrath to a hope of glory, is the greatest that can be imagined, and is oftentimes as sudden as

wonderful. Hence the general characteristics of young con-
verts are zeal and love. Like Israel at the Red Sea, they have
just seen the wonderful works of the Lord, and they cannot
but sing his praise; they are deeply affected with the danger
they have lately escaped, and with the case of multitudes
around them, who are secure and careless in the same alarming
situation! and a sense of their own mercies, and a compassion
for the souls of others, is so transporting that they can hardly
forbear preaching to every one they meet.

This emotion is highly just and reasonable, with respect to
the causes from whence it springs; and it is doubtless a proof,
not only of the imperfection, but the depravity of our nature,
that we are not always thus affected;—yet it is not entirely
genuine. If we examine this character closely, which seems at
first sight a pattern and a reproof to Christians of longer standing, we shall for the most part find it attended with considerable defects.

1. Such persons are very weak in faith. Their confidence
arises rather from the lively impressions of joy within, than
from a distinct and clear apprehension of the work of God
in Christ. The comforts which are intended as *cordials* to
animate them against the opposition of an unbelieving world,
they mistake and rest in as the *proper evidences* of their hope.
And hence it comes to pass, that when the Lord varies his dispensations, and hides his face, they are soon troubled and at
their wit's end.

2. They who are in this state of their first love, are seldom
free from something of a censorious spirit. They have not yet
felt all the deceitfulness of their own hearts; they are not well
acquainted with the devices or temptations of Satan; and
therefore know not how to sympathize or make allowances,
where allowances are necessary and due, and can hardly bear
with any who do not discover the same earnestness as themselves.

3. They are likewise, more or less under the influence of
self-righteousness and self-will. They mean well; but not
being as yet well acquainted with the spiritual meaning and
proper use of the law, nor established in the life of faith, a
part (oftentimes a very considerable part) of their zeal spends

itself in externals and non-essentials, prompts them to practise what is not commanded, to refrain from what is lawful, and to observe various and needless austerities and singularities, as their tempers and circumstances differ.

However, with all their faults, methinks there is something very beautiful and engaging in the honest vehemence of a young convert. Some cold and rigid judges are ready to reject these promising appearances on account of incidental blemishes. But would a gardener throw away a fine nectarine, because it is *green*, and has not yet attained all that beauty and flavour which a few more showers and suns will impart? Perhaps it will hold for the most part in grace as in nature (some exceptions there are), if there is not some *fire* in youth, we can hardly expect a proper warmth in old age.

But the great and good Husbandman watches over what his own hand has planted, and carries on his work by a variety of different and even contrary dispensations. While their mountain stands thus strong, they think they shall never be moved; but at length they find a change. Sometimes it comes on by insensible degrees. That part of their affection which was purely natural, will abate of course when the power of novelty ceases: they will begin, in some instances, to perceive their own indiscretions; and an endeavour to correct the excesses of an imprudent zeal will often draw them towards the contrary extreme of remissness: the evils of their hearts, which, though overpowered, were not eradicated, will revive again: the enemy will watch his occasions to meet them with suitable temptations; and as it is the Lord's design that they should experimentally learn and feel their own weakness, he will in some instances be permitted to succeed. When guilt is thus brought upon the conscience, the heart grows hard, the hands feeble, and the knees weak; then confidence is shaken, the spirit of prayer interrupted, the armour gone, and thus things grow worse and worse, till the Lord is pleased to interpose: for though we can fall of ourselves, we cannot rise without his help. Indeed every sin, in its own nature, has a tendency towards a final apostasy; but there is a provision in the covenant of grace, and the Lord, in his own time, returns to convince, humble, pardon, comfort, and renew the soul. He touches the rock, and the waters flow. By repeated experiments and exercises of this sort (for this wisdom is seldom acquired by one or a few lessons), we begin at length to learn that we are nothing, have nothing, can do nothing but sin. And thus we are gradually prepared to live more out of ourselves, and to derive all our sufficiency of every kind from Jesus, the fountain of grace. We learn to tread more warily, to trust less to our own strength, to have lower thoughts of ourselves, and higher thoughts of *him* : in which two last particulars, I apprehend what the Scripture means by a growth of grace does properly consist. Both are increasing in the lively Christian;—every day shows him more of his own heart, and more of the power, sufficiency, compassion, and grace of his adorable Redeemer; but neither will be complete till we get to heaven.

I apprehend, therefore, that though we find an abatement of that sensible warmth of affection which we felt at first setting out;— yet if our views are more evangelical, our judgement more ripened, our hearts more habitually humbled under a sense of inward depravity, our tempers more softened into sympathy and tenderness; if our prevailing desires are spiritual, and we practically esteem the precepts, ordinances, and people of God; we may warrantably conclude, that his good work of grace in us is, upon the whole, on an increase.

But still it is to be lamented, that an increase of knowledge and experience should be so generally attended with a decline of fervour. If it was not for what has passed in my own heart, I should be ready to think it impossible. But this very circumstance gives me a still more emphatical conviction of my own vileness and depravity. The want of humiliation humbles me, and my very indifference rouses and awakens me to earnestness. There are, however, seasons of refreshment, ineffable glances of light and power upon the soul, which, as they are derived from clearer displays of divine grace, if not so tumultuous as the first joys, are more penetrating, transforming, and animating. A glance of these, when compared with our sluggish stupidity when they are withheld, weans the heart from this wretched state of sin and temptation, and makes the thoughts of death and eternity desirable. Then this conflict shall cease;—I shall sin and wander no more, see him as he is, and be like him for ever.

If the question is, How are these bright moments to be prolonged, renewed, or retrieved? we are directed to faith and diligence. A careful use of the appointed means of grace, a watchful endeavour to avoid the occasions and appearances of evil, and especially assiduity in secret prayer, will bring us as much of them as the Lord sees good for us. He knows best why we are not to be trusted with them continually. Here we are to walk by faith, to be exercised and tried; by and by we shall be crowned, and the desires he has given shall be abundantly satisfied.

I am, &c.

LETTER XXI

Difference between Acquired and Experimental Knowledge.

My Lord,

I SHALL embrace your permission to fill my paper.—As to subject, that which has been a frequent theme of my heart of late, I shall venture to lay before your Lordship,—I mean the remarkable and humbling difference which I suppose all who know themselves may observe, between their acquired and their experimental knowledge, or, in other words, between their judgement and their practice. To hear a believer speak his apprehensions of the evil of sin, the vanity of the world, the love of Christ, the beauty of holiness, or the importance of eternity, who would not suppose him proof against temptation? To hear with what strong arguments he can recommend watchfulness, prayer, forbearance, and submission, when he is teaching or advising others, who would not suppose but he could also teach himself, and influence his own conduct? Yet, alas! *Quam dispar sibi!* The person who rose from his knees before he left his chamber a poor, indigent, fallible, dependent creature, who saw and acknowledged that he was unworthy to breathe the air or to see the light, may meet with many occasions before the day is closed, to discover the corruptions of his heart, and to show how weak and faint his best principles and clearest convictions are in their actual exercise. And in this view, how vain is man! what a contradiction is a believer to himself! He is called a *believer* emphatically, because he cordially assents to the word of God; but, alas! how often unworthy of the name! If I was to describe him from the Scripture-character, I should say, he is one whose heart is athirst for God, for his glory, his image, his presence: his affections are fixed upon an unseen Saviour; his treasures, and consequently his thoughts, are on high, beyond the bounds of sense. Having experienced much forgiveness, he is full of bowels of mercy to all around; and having been often deceived by his own heart, he dares trust it no more, but lives by faith in the Son of God, for wisdom, righteousness, and sanctification, and derives from him grace for grace; sensible that without him he has not sufficiency even to think a good thought. In short—he is dead to the world, to sin, to self, but alive to God, and lively in his service. Prayer is his breath, the word of God his food, and the ordinances more precious to him than the light of the sun. Such is a believer—in his judgement and prevailing desires.

But was I to describe him from experience, especially at some times, how different would the picture be! Though he knows that communion with God is his highest privilege, he too seldom finds it so; on the contrary, if duty, conscience, and necessity did not compel, he would leave the throne of grace unvisited from day to day. He takes up the Bible, conscious that it is the fountain of life and true comfort; yet perhaps while he is making the reflection, he feels a secret distaste, which prompts him to lay it down, and give his preference to a newspaper. He needs not to be told of the vanity and uncertainty of all beneath the sun; and yet is almost as much elated or cast down by a trifle, as those who have their portion in this world. He believes that all things shall work together for his good, and that the most high God appoints, adjusts, and over-rules all his concerns; yet he feels the risings of fear, anxiety, and displeasure, as though the contrary was true. He owns himself ignorant, and liable to be deceived by a thousand fallacies; yet is easily betrayed into positiveness and self-conceit. He feels himself an unprofitable, unfaithful, unthankful servant, and therefore blushes to harbour a thought of desiring the esteem and commendations of men, yet he cannot suppress it. Finally (for I must observe some bounds), on account of these and many other inconsistencies, he is struck dumb before the Lord, stripped of every hope and plea, but what is provided in the free grace of God, and yet his heart is continually leaning and returning to a covenant of works.

Two questions naturally arise from such a view of ourselves. First,—How can these things be, or why are they permitted? Since the Lord hates sin, teaches his people to hate it and cry against it, and has promised to hear their prayers, how is it that they go thus burdened? Surely if he could not, or would not, over-rule evil for good, he would not permit it to continue. By these exercises he teaches us more truly to know and feel the utter depravity and corruption of our whole nature, that we are indeed defiled in every part. His method of salvation is likewise hereby exceedingly endeared to us; we see that it is and must be of grace, wholly of grace; and that the Lord Jesus Christ, and his perfect righteousness, is and must be our all in all. His power likewise in maintaining his own work, notwithstanding our infirmities, temptations, and enemies, is hereby displayed in the clearest light, his strength is manifested in our weakness. Satan likewise is more remarkably disappointed and put to shame, when he finds bounds set to his rage and policy, beyond which he cannot pass; and that those in whom he finds so much to work upon, and over whom he so often prevails for a season, escape at last out of his hands. He casts them down, but they are raised again; he wounds them, but they are healed: he obtains his desire to sift them as wheat, but the prayer of their great Advocate prevails for the maintenance of their faith. Further, by what believers feel in themselves they learn by degrees how to warn, pity, and bear with others. A soft, patient, and compassionate spirit, and a readiness and skill in comforting those who are cast down, is not perhaps attainable in any other way. And lastly, I believe nothing more habitually reconciles a child of God to the thought of death, than the wearisomeness of this warfare. Death is unwelcome to nature;—but then, and not till then, the conflict will cease. Then we shall sin no more. The flesh, with all its attendant evils, will be laid in the grave;—then the soul, which has been partaker of a new and heavenly birth, shall be freed from every incumbrance, and stand perfect in the Redeemer's righteousness before God in glory.

But though these evils cannot be wholly removed, it is worth while to inquire, Secondly, How they may be mitigated? This we are encouraged to hope for. The word of God directs and animates to a growth in grace: and though we can do nothing spiritually of ourselves, yet there is a part assigned us. We cannot conquer the obstacles in our way by our own strength; yet we *can* give way to them; and if we do, it is our sin, and will be our sorrow. The disputes concerning inherent power in the creature, have been carried to inconvenient lengths; for my own part, I think it safe to use Scriptural language.—The apostles exhort us, to give all diligence, to resist the devil, to purge ourselves from all filthiness of flesh and spirit, to give ourselves to reading, meditation, and prayer; to watch, to put on the whole armour of God, and to abstain from all appearance of evil. Faithfulness to light received, and a sincere endeavour to conform to the means prescribed in the word of God, with an humble application to the blood of sprinkling, and the promised Spirit, will undoubtedly be answered by increasing measures of light, faith, strength, and comfort; and we shall know, if we follow on to know the Lord.

I need not tell your Lordship that I am an extempore writer. I dropped the consideration of whom I was addressing from the first paragraph; but I now return and subscribe myself, with the greatest deference, &c.

LETTER XXII

The Believer's Inability on Account of Remaining Sin.

My Lord,

I HAVE been sitting perhaps a quarter of an hour with my pen in my hand, and my finger upon my upper lip, contriving how I should begin my letter.—A detail of the confused incoherent thoughts which have successively passed through my mind, would have more than filled the sheet; but your Lordship's patience and even your charity for the writer, would have been tried to the uttermost, if I could have penned them all down. At length my suspense reminded me of the apostle's words, Gal. v. 17. "Ye cannot do the things that ye would." This is an humbling but a just account of a Christian's attainments in the present life, and is equally applicable to the strongest and to the weakest. The weakest need not say *less,* the strongest will hardly venture to say *more.* The Lord has given his people a desire and will aiming at great things; without this they would be unworthy the name of Christians; but they cannot do as they would: their best desires are weak and ineffectual, not absolutely so (for he who works in them to will, enables them in a measure to do likewise), but in comparison with the mark at which they aim. So that while they have great cause to be thankful for the desire he has given them, and for the degree in which it is answered, they have equal reason to be ashamed and abased under a sense of their continual defects, and the evil mixtures which taint and debase their best endeavours. It would be easy to make out a long list of particulars which a believer would do if he could, but in which, from first to last, he finds a mortifying inability. Permit me to mention a few, which I need not transcribe from books, for they are always present to my mind.

He would willingly enjoy God in prayer:—he knows that

prayer is his duty; but, in his judgement, he considers it likewise as his greatest honour and privilege. In this light he can
recommend it to others, and can tell them of the wonderful
condescension of the great God, who humbles himself to behold
the things that are in heaven, that he should stoop so much
lower, to afford his gracious ear to the supplications of sinful
worms upon earth. He can bid them expect a pleasure in
waiting upon the Lord, different in kind and greater in degree
than all that the world can afford. By prayer he can say, You
have liberty to cast all your cares upon him that careth for
you. By one hour's intimate access to the throne of grace,
where the Lord causes his glory to pass before the soul that
seeks him, you may acquire more true spiritual knowledge and
comfort, than by a day or a week's converse with the best of
men, or the most studious perusal of many folios: and in this
light he would consider it and improve it for himself. But
alas! how seldom can he do as he would! How often does he
find this privilege a mere task, which he would be glad of a
just excuse to omit? and the chief pleasure he derives from
the performance is to think that his task is finished:—he has
been drawing near to God with his lips, while his heart was
far from him. Surely this is not doing as he would, when (to
borrow the expression of an old woman here) he is dragged
before God like a slave, and comes away like a thief.

The like may be said of reading the Scripture. He believes
it to be the word of God: he admires the wisdom and grace of
the doctrines, the beauty of the precepts, the richness and
suitableness of the promises; and therefore, with David, he
accounts it preferable to thousands of gold and silver, and
sweeter than honey or the honeycomb. Yet while he thus
thinks of it, and desires that it may dwell in him richly, and
be his meditation night and day, he cannot do as he would. It
will require some resolution to persist in reading a portion of
it every day; and even then his heart is often less engaged than
when reading a pamphlet. Here again his privilege frequently
dwindles into a task. His appetite is vitiated, so that he has
but little relish for the food of his soul.

He would willingly have abiding, admiring thoughts of the
person and love of the Lord Jesus Christ. Glad he is, indeed,

of those occasions which recall the Saviour to his mind; and with this view, notwithstanding all discouragements, he perseveres in attempting to pray and read, and waits upon the ordinances. Yet he cannot do as he would. Whatever claims he may have to the exercise of gratitude and sensibility towards his fellow-creatures, he must confess himself mournfully ungrateful and insensible towards his best Friend and Benefactor. Ah! what trifles are capable of shutting *him* out of our thoughts, of whom we say, He is the Beloved of our souls, who loved us, and gave himself for us, and whom we have deliberately chosen as our chief good and portion. What can make us amends for the loss we suffer here? Yet surely if we *could*, we *would* set him always before us; his love should be the delightful theme of our hearts

From morn to noon, from noon to dewy eve.

But though we aim at this good, evil is present with us; we find we are renewed but in part, and have still cause to plead the Lord's promise to take away the heart of stone and give us a heart of flesh.

He would willingly acquiesce in all the dispensations of Divine Providence. He believes that all events are under the direction of infinite wisdom and goodness, and shall surely issue in the glory of God and the good of those who fear him. He doubts not but the hairs of his head are all numbered, that the blessings of every kind which he possesses, were bestowed upon him, and are preserved to him, by the bounty and special favour of the Lord whom he serves;—that afflictions spring not out of the ground, but are fruits and tokens of Divine love, no less than his comforts;—that there is a need-be, whenever for a season he is in heaviness. Of these principles he can no more doubt, than of what he sees with his eyes, and there are seasons when he thinks they will prove sufficient to reconcile him to the sharpest trials. But often when he aims to apply them in an hour of *present* distress, he cannot do what he would. He feels a law in his members warring against the law in his mind; so that, in defiance of the clearest convictions, seeing as though he perceived not, he is ready to complain, murmur, and despond. Alas! how vain is man in his best estate! How much weakness and inconsistency even in those whose hearts are right with the Lord! and what reason have we to confess that we are unworthy, unprofitable servants!

It were easy to enlarge in this way, would paper and time permit. But blessed be God, we are not under the law, but under grace. And even these distressing effects of the remnants of indwelling sin are over-ruled for good. By these experiences the believer is weaned more from self, and taught more highly to prize and more absolutely to rely on him, who is appointed unto us of God, Wisdom, Righteousness, Sanctification, and Redemption. The more vile we are in our own eyes, the more precious he will be to us; and a deep repeated sense of the evil of our hearts is necessary to preclude all boasting, and to make us willing to give the whole glory of our salvation where it is due. Again, a sense of these evils will (when hardly anything else can do it) reconcile us to the thoughts of death; yea, make us desirous to depart that we may sin no more, since we find depravity so deep rooted in our nature, that (like the leprous house) the whole fabric must be taken down before we can be freed from its defilement. Then, and not till then, we shall be able to do the thing that we would: when we see Jesus, we shall be transformed into his image, and have done with sin and sorrow for ever.

I am, with great deference, &c.

LETTER XXIII

Evil Present with the Believer.

My Lord,

I THINK my last letter turned upon the apostle's thought, Gal. v. 17. "Ye cannot do the things that ye would." In the parallel place, Rom. vii. 19 there is another clause subjoined, "The evil which I would not, that I do." This, added to the former, would complete the dark side of my experience.

Permit me to tell your Lordship a little part (for some things must not, cannot be told), not of what I have read, but of what I have felt, in illustration of this passage.

I *would not* be the sport and prey of wild, vain, foolish, and worse imaginations; but this evil is present with me: my heart is like a highway, like a city without walls or gates. Nothing so false, so frivolous, so absurd, so impossible, or so horrid, but it can obtain access, and that at any time, or in any place: neither the study, the pulpit, or even the Lord's table, exempt me from their intrusion. I sometimes compare my *words* to the treble of an instrument, which my *thoughts* accompany with a kind of base, or rather anti-base, in which every rule of harmony is broken, every possible combination of discord and confusion is introduced, utterly inconsistent with, and contradictory to, the intended melody. Ah! what music would my praying and preaching often make in the ears of the Lord of Hosts, if he listened to them as they are *mine* only! By men, the upper part only (if I may so speak) is heard; and small cause there is for self-gratulation, if *they* should happen to commend, when conscience tells me they would be struck with astonishment and abhorrence could they hear the whole.

But if this awful effect of heart-depravity cannot be wholly avoided in the present state of human nature, yet, at least, I would not allow and indulge it; yet this I find I do. In defiance of my best judgement and best wishes, I find something within me which cherishes and cleaves to those evils, from which I ought to start and flee, as I should if a toad or a serpent was put in my food or in my bed. Ah! how vile must the heart (at least my heart) be, that can hold a parley with such abominations, when I so well know their nature and their tendency. Surely he who finds himself capable of this, may, without the least affectation of humility (however fair his outward conduct appears), subscribe himself less than the least of all saints, and of sinners the very chief.

I would not be influenced by a principle of self on any occasion; yet this evil I often do. I see the baseness and absurdity of such a conduct as clearly as I see the light of the day. I do not affect to be thought ten feet high, and I know that a desire of being thought wise or good, is equally contrary to reason and truth. I should be grieved or angry if my fellow-creatures supposed I had such a desire; and therefore I fear the very principle of self, of which I complain, has a considerable share in prompting my desires to conceal it. The pride of others often offends me, and makes me studious to hide my own; because their good opinion of me depends much upon their not perceiving it. But the Lord knows how this dead fly taints and spoils my best services, and makes them no better than specious sins.

I would not indulge vain reasonings concerning the counsels, ways, and providences of God; yet I am prone to do it. That the Judge of all the earth will do right, is to me as evident and necessary as that two and two make four. I believe that he has a sovereign right to do what he will with his own, and that this sovereignty is but another name for the unlimited exercise of wisdom and goodness. But my reasonings are often such, as if I had never heard of these principles, or had formally renounced them. I feel the workings of a presumptuous spirit that would account for everything, and venture to dispute whatever it cannot comprehend. What an evil is this, for a potsherd of the earth to contend with its Maker! I do not act thus towards my fellow-creatures; I do not find fault with the decisions of a judge, or the dispositions of a general, because, though I know they are fallible, yet I suppose they are wiser in their respective departments than myself. But I am often ready to take this liberty when it is most unreasonable and inexcusable.

I would not cleave to a covenant of works: it should seem from the foregoing particulars, and many others which I could mention, that I have reasons enough to deter me from this. Yet even this I do. Not but that I say—and I hope from my heart—Enter not into judgement with thy servant, O Lord. I embrace it as a faithful saying, and worthy of all acceptation, that Jesus Christ came into the world to save sinners; and it is the main pleasure and business of my life to set forth the necessity and all-sufficiency of the Mediator between God and man, and to make mention of his righteousness even of his only. But here, as in everything else, I find a vast difference between my judgement and my experience. I am invited to take the water of life *freely*, yet often discouraged, because I have nothing wherewith to pay for it. If I am at times favoured with some liberty from the above-mentioned evils, it rather gives me a more favourable opinion of myself, than increases my admiration of the Lord's goodness to so unworthy a creature; and when the returning tide of my corruptions convinces me that *I am still the same*, an unbelieving legal spirit would urge me to conclude that the Lord is changed: at least, I feel a weariness of being beholden to him for such continued multiplied forgiveness; and I fear that some part of my striving against sin, and my desires after an increase of sanctification, arises from a secret wish that I might not be so absolutely and entirely indebted to him.

This, my Lord, is only a faint sketch of my heart; but it is taken from the life: it would require a volume rather than a letter to fill up the outlines. But I believe you will not regret that I choose to say no more upon such a subject. But though my disease is grievous, it is not desperate; I have a gracious and infallible Physician. I shall not die, but live, and declare the works of the Lord.

I remain, my Lord, &c.

LETTER XXIV

Advantages from Remaining Sin.

My Lord,

MY last two letters turned upon a mournful subject, the depravity of the heart, which impedes us when we would do good, and pollutes our best intended services with evil. We have cause, upon this account, to go softly all our days; yet we need not sorrow as they who have no hope. The Lord has provided his people relief under those complaints, and teaches us to draw improvement from them. If the evils we feel were not capable of being over-ruled for good, he would not permit them to remain in us. This we may infer from his hatred to sin, and the love which he bears to his people.

As to the remedy, neither our state nor his honour are affected by the workings of indwelling sin, in the hearts of those whom he has taught to wrestle, strive, and mourn, on account of what they feel. Though sin wars, it shall not reign; and though it breaks our peace, it cannot separate from his love. Nor is it inconsistent with his holiness and perfection, to manifest his favour to such poor defiled creatures, or to admit them to communion with himself; for they are not considered as in themselves, but as one with Jesus, to whom they have fled for refuge, and by whom they live a life of faith. They are accepted in the Beloved, they have an Advocate with the Father, who once made an atonement for their sins, and ever lives to make intercession for their persons. Though they cannot fulfil the law, he has fulfilled it for them; though the obedience of the members is defiled and imperfect, the obedience of the Head is spotless and complete; and though there is much evil in them, there is something good, the fruit of his own gracious Spirit. They act from a principle of love, they aim at no less than his glory, and their habitual desires are supremely fixed upon himself. There is a difference in kind between the feeblest efforts of faith in a real believer, while he is covered with shame at the thoughts of his miscarriages, and the highest and most specious attainments of those who are wise in their own eyes, and prudent in their own sight. Nor shall this conflict remain long, or the enemy finally prevail over them. They are supported by almighty power, and led on to certain victory. They shall not always be as they are now; yet a little while, and they shall be freed from this vile body, which, like the leprous house, is incurably contaminated, and must be entirely taken down. Then they shall see Jesus as he is, and be like him, and with him for ever.

The gracious purposes to which the Lord makes the sense and feeling of our depravity subservient, are manifold. Hereby his own power, wisdom, faithfulness, and love, are more signally displayed—his power, in maintaining his own work in the midst of so much opposition, like a spark burning in the water, or a bush unconsumed in the flames; his wisdom, in defeating and controlling all the devices which Satan, from his knowledge of the evil of our nature, is encouraged to practise against us. He has overthrown many a fair professor, and, like Goliath, he challenges the whole army of Israel; yet he finds there are some against whom, though he thrusts sorely, he cannot prevail; notwithstanding any seeming advantage he gains at some seasons, they are still delivered, for the Lord is on their side. The unchangeableness of the Lord's love, and the riches of his mercy, are likewise more illustrated by the multiplied pardons he bestows upon his people, than if they needed no forgiveness at all.

Hereby the Lord Jesus Christ is more endeared to the soul; all boasting is effectually excluded, and the glory of a full and free salvation is ascribed to him alone. If a mariner is surprised by a storm, and after one night spent in jeopardy, is presently brought safe into port; though he may rejoice in his deliverance, it will not affect him so sensibly, as if, after being tempest-tossed for a long season, and experiencing a great number and variety of hair-breadth escapes, he at last gains the desired haven. The righteous are said to be scarcely saved, not with respect to the certainty of the event, for the purpose of God in their favour cannot be disappointed, but in respect of their own apprehensions, and the great difficulties they are brought through. But when, after a long experience of their own deceitful hearts, after repeated proofs of their weakness, wilfulness, ingratitude, and insensibility, they find that none of these things can separate them from the love of God in Christ, Jesus becomes more and more precious to their souls. They love much, because much has been forgiven them. They dare not, they will not ascribe anything to themselves, but are glad to acknowledge, that they must have perished (if possible) a thousand times over, if Jesus had not been their Saviour, their shepherd, and their shield. When they were wandering he brought them back, when fallen he raised them, when wounded he healed them, when fainting he revived them. By him out of weakness they have been made strong; he has taught their hands to war, and covered their heads in the day of battle. In a word, some of the clearest proofs they have had of his excellence, have been occasioned by the mortifying proofs they have had of their own vileness. They would not have known so much of them, if they had not known so much of themselves.

Further, a spirit of humiliation, which is both the *Decus et Tutamen*, the strength and beauty of our profession, is greatly promoted by our feeling, as well as reading, that when we would do good, evil is present with us. A broken and contrite spirit is pleasing to the Lord who has promised to dwell with those who have it; and experience shows, that the exercise of all our graces is in proportion to the humbling sense we have of the depravity of our nature. But that we are so totally depraved, is a truth which no one ever truly learned by being only told it. Indeed if we could receive, and habitually maintain, a right judgement of ourselves, by what is plainly declared in Scripture, it would probably save us many a mournful hour; but experience is the Lord's school, and they who are taught by him usually learn, that they have no wisdom by the mistakes they make, and that they have no strength by the slips and falls they meet with. Every day draws forth some new corruption which before was little observed, or at least discovers it in a stronger light than before. Thus by degrees they are weaned from leaning to any supposed wisdom, power, or goodness in themselves; they feel the truth of our Lord's words, "Without me ye can do nothing;" and the necessity of crying with David, "O lead me and guide me for they name's sake." It is chiefly by this frame of mind that one Christian is differenced from another; for, though it is an inward feeling, it has very observable outward effects, which are expressively intimated, Ezek. xvi. 63. "Thou shalt be dumb and not open thy mouth, in the day when I am pacified towards thee, saith the Lord God." The knowledge of my full and free forgiveness of thy innumerable backslidings and transgressions, shall make thee ashamed, and silence the unruly workings of thine heart. Thou shalt open thy mouth in praise; but thou shalt no more boast in thyself, or censure others, or repine at my dispensations. In these respects we are exceedingly prone to speak unadvisedly with our lips. But a sense of great unworthiness and much forgiveness checks these evils. Whoever is truly humbled will not be easily angry, will not be positive

and rash, will be compassionate and tender to the infirmities
of his fellow-sinners, knowing, that if there be a difference, it
is grace that has made it, and that he has the seeds of every
evil in his own heart; and, under all trials and afflictions, he
will look to the hand of the Lord, and lay his mouth in the
dust, acknowledging that he suffers much less than his iniqui-
ties have deserved.   These are some of the advantages and
good fruits which the Lord enables us to obtain from that
bitter root, indwelling sin.

I am, with great deference, &c.

LETTER XXV

What the Believer can attain to in this Life.

My Lord,

WEAK, unskilful, and unfaithful, as I am in practice, the Lord
has been pleased to give me some idea of what a Christian ought
to be, and of what is actually attainable in the present life, by
those whom he enables earnestly to aspire towards the prize of
their high calling.   They who are versed in mechanics can,
from a knowledge of the combined powers of a complicated
machine, make an exact calculation of what it is able to perform, and what resistance it can counteract; but who can com-
pute the possible effects of that combination of principles and
motives revealed in the Gospel, upon a heart duly impressed
with a sense of their importance and glory?   When I was
lately at Mr. Cox's Museum, while I was fixing my attention
upon some curious movements, imagining that I saw the whole
of the artist's design, the person who showed it touched a little
spring, and suddenly a thousand new and unexpected motions
took place, and the whole piece seemed animated from the top
to the bottom.   I should have formed but a very imperfect
judgement of it, had I seen no more than what I saw at first.
I thought it might in some measure illustrate the vast difference
that is observable amongst professors, even amongst those who

are, it is to be hoped, sincere. There are persons who appear to have a true knowledge (in part) of the nature of the Gospel-religion, but seem not to be apprised of its properties, in their comprehension and extent. If they have attained to some hope of their acceptance, if they find at seasons some communion with God in the means of grace, if they are in measure delivered from the prevailing and corrupt customs of the world, they seem to be satisfied, as if they were possessed of all. These are indeed great things; *Sed meliora latent*. The profession of too many, whose sincerity charity would be unwilling to impeach, is greatly blemished, notwithstanding their hopes and their occasional comforts, by the breakings forth of unsanctified tempers, and the indulgence of vain hopes, anxious cares, and selfish pursuits. Far, very far, am I from that unscriptural sentiment of sinless perfection in fallen man. To those who have a due sense of the spirituality and ground of the divine precepts, and of what passes in their own hearts, there will never be wanting causes of humiliation and self-abasement on the account of sin; yet still there is a liberty and privilege attainable by the Gospel, beyond what is ordinarily thought of. Permit me to mention two or three particulars, in which those who have a holy ambition of aspiring to them shall not be altogether disappointed.

I. A delight in the Lord's all-sufficiency, to be satisfied in him as our present and eternal portion. This, in the sense in which I understand it, is not the effect of a present warm frame, but of a deeply-rooted and abiding principle, the habitual exercise of which is to be estimated by the comparative indifference with which other things are regarded. The soul thus principled is not at leisure to take or to seek satisfaction in anything but what has a known subserviency to this leading taste. Either the Lord is present, and then he is to be rejoiced in; or else he is absent, and then he is to be sought and waited for. They are to be pitied, who, if they are at some times happy in the Lord, can at other times be happy without him, and rejoice in broken cisterns, when their spirits are at a distance from the fountain of living waters. I do not plead for an absolute in-difference to temporal blessings; he gives us all things richly to *enjoy*; and a capacity of relishing them is his gift likewise; but then the consideration of his love in bestowing should exceedingly enhance the value, and a regard to his will should regulate their use. Nor can they all supply the want of *that* which we can only receive immediately from himself. This principle likewise moderates that inordinate fear and sorrow to which we are liable upon the prospect or the occurrence of great trials, for which there is a sure support and resource provided in the all-sufficiency of infinite goodness and grace. What a privilege is this, to possess God *in all things* while we have them, and all things in God when they are taken from us!

II. An acquiescence in the Lord's will founded in a persuasion of his wisdom, holiness, sovereignty, and goodness. This is one of the greatest privileges and brightest ornaments of our profession. So far as we attain to this, we are secure from disappointment. Our own limited views, and short-sighted purposes and desires, may be, and will be, often over-ruled; but then our main and leading desire, that the will of the Lord may be done, must be accomplished. How highly does it become us, both as creatures and as sinners, to submit to the appointments of our Maker! and how necessary is it to our peace! This great attainment is too often unthought of, and overlooked; we are prone to fix our attention upon the second causes and immediate instruments of events; forgetting that whatever befalls us is according to his purpose, and therefore must be right and seasonable in itself, and shall in the issue be productive of good. From hence arise impatience, resentment, and secret repinings, which are not only sinful, but tormenting; whereas, if all things are in his hand, if the very hairs of our head are numbered; if every event, great and small, is under the direction of his providence and purpose; and if he has a wise, holy, and gracious end in view, to which everything that happens is subordinate and subservient;—then we have nothing to do, but with patience and humility to follow as he leads, and cheerfully to expect a happy issue. The path of present duty is marked out; and the concerns of the next and every succeeding hour are in his hands. How happy are they who can resign all to him, see his hand in every dispensation, and believe that he chooses better for them than they possibly could for themselves!

III. A single eye to his glory, as the ultimate scope of all our undertakings. The Lord can design nothing short of his own glory, nor should we. The constraining love of Christ has a direct and marvellous tendency, in proportion to the measure of faith, to mortify the corrupt principle, *Self*, which for a season is the grand spring of our conduct, and by which we are too much biassed after we know the Lord. But as grace prevails, self is renounced. We feel that we are not our own, that we are bought with a price; and that it is our duty, our honour, and our happiness, to be the servants of God and of the Lord Jesus Christ. To devote soul and body, every talent, power, and faculty, to the service of his cause and will; to let our light shine (in our several situations) to the praise of his grace; to place our highest joy in the contemplation of his adorable perfections; to rejoice even in tribulations and distresses, in reproaches and infirmities, if thereby the power of Christ may rest upon us, and be magnified in us; to be content, yea, glad to be nothing, that he may be all in all;—to obey *him*, in opposition to the threats or solicitations of men; to trust *him*, though all outward appearances seem against us; to rejoice in *him*, though we should (as will sooner or later be the case) have nothing else to rejoice in;—to live above the world, and to have our conversation in heaven, to be like the angels, finding our own pleasure in performing his :—This, my lord, is the prize, the mark of our high calling, to which we are encouraged with a holy ambition continually to aspire. It is true, we shall still fall short; we shall find, that when we would do good, evil will be present with us. But the attempt is glorious, and shall not be wholly in vain. He that gives us thus *to will*, will enable us to perform with growing success, and teach us to profit even by our mistakes and imperfections.

O blessed man! that thus fears the Lord, that delights in his word, and derives his principles, motives, maxims, and consolations, from that unfailing source of light and strength. He shall be like a tree planted by the rivers of water, whose leaf is always green, and fruit abundant. The wisdom that is above shall direct his plans, inspire his counsels; and the power of God shall guard him on every side, and prepare his way through every difficulty: he shall see mountains sink into plains, and streams spring up in the dry wilderness. The Lord's enemies will be his; and they may be permitted to fight against him, but they shall not prevail, for the Lord is with him to deliver him. The conduct of such a one, though in a narrow and retired sphere of life, is of more real excellence and importance, than the most splendid actions of kings and conquerors, which fill the annals of history, Prov. xvi. 32. And if the God whom he serves is pleased to place him in a more public light, his labours and cares will be amply compensated, by the superior opportunities afforded him of manifesting the power and reality of true religion, and promoting the good of mankind.

I hope I *may* say that I *desire* to be thus entirely given up to the Lord; I am sure I *must* say, that what I have written is far from being my actual experience. Alas! I might be condemned out of my own mouth, were the Lord strict to mark what is amiss. But, O the comfort! we are not under the law, but under grace. The Gospel is a dispensation for sinners, and we have an Advocate with the Father. *There* is the unshaken ground of hope. A reconciled Father, a prevailing Advocate, a powerful Shepherd, a compassionate Friend, a Saviour who is able and willing to save to the uttermost. He knows our frame; he remembers that we are but dust; and has opened for us a new and blood-besprinkled way of access to the throne of grace, that we may obtain mercy, and find grace to help in every time of need.

I am, &c.

LETTER XXVI

The Greatness of God.

My Lord,

THE first line of Horace's epistle to Augustus, when rightly applied, suggests a grand and cheering idea. As addressed by the poet, nothing can be more blasphemous, idolatrous, and absurd; but with what comfort and propriety may a Christian look up to Him, to whom all power is committed in heaven and earth, and say, *Cum tot sustineas et tanta negotia solus!*[1] Surely a more weighty and comprehensive sentence never dropped from an uninspired pen. And how beautifully and expressively is it closed by the word *solus!* The government is upon his shoulders; and though he is concealed by a veil of second causes from common eyes, so that they can perceive only the means, instruments, and contingencies by which he works, and therefore think he does nothing; yet, in reality, he does *all*, according to his own counsel and pleasure, in the armies of heaven, and among the inhabitants of the earth.

Who can enumerate the *Tot et tanta negotia*,[2] which are incessantly before his eye, adjusted by his wisdom, dependent on his will, and regulated by his power, in his kingdoms of providence and grace? If we consider the heavens, the work of his fingers, the moon and the stars which he has ordained; if we call in the assistance of astronomers and glasses to help us in forming a conception of the number, distances, magnitudes, and motions of the heavenly bodies; the more we search, the more we shall be confirmed, that these are but a portion of his ways.—But he calls them all by their names, upholds them by his power, and without his continual energy they would rush into confusion, or sink into nothing. If we speak of intelligences, he is the life, the joy, the sun of all that are capable of happiness. Whatever may be signified by the thrones, principalities, and powers in the world of light, they are all dependent upon his power, and obedient to his command; it is equally true of angels as of men, that without him they can do nothing. The powers of darkness are likewise under his subjection and control. Though but little is said of them in Scripture, we read enough to assure us that their number must be immensely great, and that their strength, subtlety, and malice are such, as we may tremble to think of them as our enemies, and probably should, but for our strange insensibility to whatever does not fall under the cognisance of our outward senses.

---

[1] You alone uphold so many and great labours.
[2] So many and great labours.

But he holds them all in a chain, so that they can do or attempt nothing but by his permission; and whatever he permits them to do (though they mean nothing less) has its appointed sub-serviency in accomplishing his designs.

But to come nearer home, and to speak of what seems more suited to our scanty apprehensions,—still we may be lost in wonder. Before this blessed and only Potentate, all the nations of the earth are but as the dust upon the balance, and the small drop of a bucket, and might be thought (if compared with the immensity of his works) scarcely worthy of his notice: yet here he presides, pervades, provides, protects, and rules. In him his creatures live, move, and have their being: from him is their food and preservation. The eyes of all are upon him: what he gives they gather, and can gather no more; and at his word they sink into the dust. There is not a worm that crawls upon the ground, or a flower that grows in the pathless wilder-ness, or a shell upon the sea shore, but bears the impress of his wisdom, power, and goodness. With respect to men, he reigns with uncontrolled dominion over every kingdom, family, and individual. Here we may be astonished at his wisdom in employing free agents, the greater part of whom are his enemies, to accomplish his purposes. But, however reluctant, they all serve him. His patience likewise is wonderful. Multi-tudes, yea nearly our whole species, spend the life and strength which he affords them, and abuse all the bounties he heaps upon them, in the ways of sin. His commands are disre-garded, his name blasphemed, his mercy disdained, his power defied, yet still he spares. It is an eminent part of his govern-ment, to restrain the depravity of human nature, and in vari-ous ways to check its effects, which if left to itself, without his providential control, would presently make earth the very image of hell. For the vilest men are not suffered to perpe-trate a thousandth part of the evil which their hearts would prompt them to. The earth, though lying in the wicked one, is filled with the goodness of the Lord. He preserveth man and beast, sustains the young lion in the forest, feeds the birds of the air, which have neither storehouse nor barn, and adorns the insects and the flowers of the field with a beauty and elegance beyond all that can be found in the courts of kings.

Still more wonderful is his administration in his kingdom of grace. He is present with all his creatures, but in a peculiar manner with his own people. All of these are monuments of a more illustrious display of power, than that which spread abroad the heavens like a curtain, and laid the foundations of the earth: for he finds them all in a state of rebellion and enmity, and makes them a willing people; and from the moment he reveals his love to them, he espouses their cause, and takes all their concerns into his own hands. He is near and attentive to every one of them, as if there was only that one. This high and lofty One, who inhabits eternity, before whom the angels veil their faces, condescends to hold communion with those whom men despise. He sees not as man seeth—rides on a cloud disdainful by a sultan or a czar, to manifest himself to a humble soul in a mud-walled cottage. He comforts them when in trouble, strengthens them when weak, makes their beds in sickness, revives them when fainting, upholds them when falling, and so seasonably and effectually manages for them, that though they are persecuted and tempted, though their enemies are many and mighty, nothing that they feel or fear is able to separate them from his love.

And all this He does *solus*. All the abilities, powers, and instincts, that are found amongst creatures, are emanations from his fulness. All changes, successes, disappointments—all that is memorable in the annals of history, all the risings and falls of empires, all the turns in human life, take place according to his plan. In vain men contrive and combine to accomplish their own counsels. Unless they are parts of his counsel likewise, the efforts of their utmost strength and wisdom are crossed and reversed by the feeblest and most unthought-of-circumstances. But when he has a work to accomplish, and his time is come, however inadequate and weak the means he employs may seem to a carnal eye, the success is infallibly secured: for all things serve him, and are in his hands as clay in the hands of the potter. Great and marvellous are thy works, Lord God Almighty! just and true are thy ways, thou King of saints!

This is the God whom we adore. This is he who invites us to lean upon his almighty arm, and promises to guide us with his unerring eye. He says to you, my lord, and even to me, "Fear not, I am with thee; be not dismayed, I am thy God; I will strengthen thee, yea I will help thee, yea I will uphold thee, with the right hand of my righteousness." Therefore, while in the path of duty, and following his call, we may cheerfully pass on, regardless of apparent difficulties; for the Lord, whose we are, and who has taught us to make his glory our highest end, will go before us, and at his word crooked things become straight, light shines out of darkness, and mountains sink into plains. Faith may and must be exercised, experience must and will confirm what his word declares, that the heart is deceitful, and that man in his best estate is vanity. But his promises to them that fear him shall be confirmed likewise, and they shall find him, in all situations, a sun, a shield, and an exceeding great reward.

I have lost another of my people; a mother in our Israel; a person of much experience, eminent grace, wisdom, and usefulness. She walked with God forty years: she was one of the Lord's poor; but her poverty was decent, sanctified, and honourable. She lived respected, and her death is considered as a public loss. It is a great loss to me: I shall miss her advice and example, by which I have been often edified and animated. But Jesus still lives. Almost her last words were, "The Lord is my portion, saith my soul."

I am, &c.

LETTER XXVII

The Lord the Shepherd of His People.

My Lord,

I HAVE not very lately had recourse to the expedient of descanting upon a text, but I believe it the best method I can take to avoid ringing changes upon a few obvious topics, which I suppose uniformly present themselves to my mind when I am about to write to your lordship. Just now that sweet expression

of David occurred to my thoughts, *The Lord is my Shepherd!*
Permit me, without plan or premeditation, to make a few
observations upon it; and may your lordship feel the peace, the
confidence, the blessedness, which a believing application of
the words is suited to inspire.

The Socinians, and others, in their unhappy laboured
attempts to darken the principal glory and foundation-comfort
of the Gospel, employ their critical sophistry against those texts
which expressly and doctrinally declare the Redeemer's character; and affect to triumph, if in any manuscript or ancient
version they can find a variation from the received copies
which seems to favour their cause. But we may venture to
waive the authority of every disputed or disputable text, and
maintain the truth against their cavils, from the current
language and tenor of the whole Scripture. David's words in
Psalm xxiii. are alone a decisive proof that Jesus is Jehovah,
if they will but allow two things, which I think they cannot
deny;—1. That our Saviour assumes to himself the character
of the Shepherd of his people;—and 2. That he did not come
into the world to abridge those advantages which the servants
of God enjoyed before his incarnation. Upon these premises,
which cannot be gainsaid without setting aside the whole
New Testament, the conclusion is undeniable: for if Jehovah
was David's Shepherd, unless Jesus be Jehovah, we who live
under the Gospel have an unspeakable disadvantage, in being
entrusted to the care of one who, according to the Socinians, is
a mere man; and, upon the Arian scheme, is at the most a
creature, and infinitely short of possessing those perfections
which David contemplated in his Shepherd. He had a Shepherd whose wisdom and power were infinite, and might therefore warrantably conclude he should not want, and need not
fear. And we also may conclude the same, if our Shepherd
be the Lord or Jehovah, but not otherwise. Besides, the very
nature of the Shepherd's office respecting the state of such
frail creatures as we are, requires those attributes for the due discharge of it, which are incommunicably divine. He must inti-
mately know every individual of the flock.—His eye must be
upon them every one, and his ear open to their prayers, and his
arm stretched out for their relief, in all places and in all ages.—

Every thought of every heart must be open to his view, and his wisdom must penetrate, and his arm control and over-rule all the hidden and complicated machinations of the powers of darkness.—He must have the administration of universal providence over all the nations, families, and persons upon earth, or he could not effectually manage for those who put their trust in him, in that immense variety of cases and circumstances in which they are found. Reason, as well as Scripture, may convince us, that he who gathereth the outcasts of Israel, who healeth the broken in heart, who upholdeth all that fall, raiseth up all that are bowed down, and upon whom the eyes of all wait for their support, can be no other than he who telleth the number of the stars, and calleth them all by their names, who is great in power, and whose understanding is infinite. To this purpose likewise the prophet Isaiah describes this mighty Shepherd, chap. xl. 9-17, both as to his person and office.

But is not this indeed the great mystery of godliness! How just is the apostle's observation, that no man can say, Jesus Christ is the Lord, but by the Holy Ghost! How astonishing the thought,—that the Maker of heaven and earth, the Holy One of Israel, before whose presence the earth shook, the heavens dropped, when he displayed a faint emblem of his majesty upon Sinai, should afterwards appear in the form of a servant, and hang upon a cross, the sport and scorn of wicked men! I cannot wonder that to the wise men of the world this appears absurd, unreasonable, and impossible; yet to right reason, to reason enlightened and sanctified, however amazing the proposition be, yet it appears true and necessary, upon a supposition that a holy God is pleased to pardon sinners in a way suited to display the awful glories of his justice. The same arguments which prove the blood of bulls and goats insufficient to take away sin, will conclude against the utmost doings or sufferings of men or angels. The Redeemer of sinners must be mighty; he must have a personal dignity to stamp such a value upon his undertakings, as that thereby God may appear just, as well as merciful, in justifying the ungodly for his sake; and he must be all-sufficient to bless, and almighty to protect, those who come unto him for safety and life.

Such a one is our Shepherd. This is he of whom we, through

grace, are enabled to say, we are *his* people, and the sheep of *his* pasture. We are his by every tie and right; he made us, he redeemed us, he reclaimed us from the hand of our enemies, and we are his by our own voluntary surrender of ourselves; for though we once slighted, despised, and opposed him, he made us willing in the day of his power: he knocked at the door of our hearts; but we (at least I) barred and fastened it against him as much and as long as possible. But when he revealed his love, we could stand out no longer. Like sheep, we are weak, destitute, defenceless, prone to wander, unable to return, and always surrounded with wolves. But all is made up in the fulness, ability, wisdom, compassion, care, and faithfulness of our great Shepherd. He guides, protects, feeds, heals, and restores, and will be our guide and our God even until death. Then he will meet us, receive us, and present us unto himself, and we shall be near him, and like him, and with him for ever.

Ah! my lord, what a subject is this! I trust it is the joy of your heart. Placed as you are by his hand in a superior rank, you see and feel that the highest honours, and the most important concernments that terminate with the present life, are trivial as the sports of children, in comparison with the views and the privileges you derive from the glorious Gospel; and your situation in life renders the grace bestowed upon you the more conspicuous and distinguishing. I have somewhere met with a similar reflection of Henry the Fourth of France, to this purpose, that though many came into the world the same day with him, he was probably the only one among them that was born to be a king. Your lordship is acquainted with many, who, if not born on the same day with you, were born to titles, estates, and honours; but how few of them were born to the honour of making a public and consistent profession of the glorious Gospel! The hour is coming when all honours and possessions, but this which cometh of God only, will be eclipsed and vanish; and, "like the baseless fabric of a vision, leave not a rack behind." How miserable will they then be, who must leave their *all*! What a mortifying thought does Horace put in the way of those who disdain to read the Scripture!

Linquenda tellus, et domus, et placens
Uxor: neque harum, quas colis, arborum
Te, præter invisas cupressos,
Ulla brevem dominum sequetur.[1]

But grace and faith can make the lowest state of life supportable, and make a dismission from the highest desirable. Of the former I have many living proofs and witnesses around me. Your lordship, I trust, will have sweet experience of the latter, when, after having fulfilled the will of God in your generation, you shall be called (I hope in some yet distant day) to enter into your Master's joy. In the meantime, how valuable are life, talents, influence, and opportunities of every kind, if we are enabled to improve and lay out all for him who has thus loved us, thus provided for us! As to myself, I would hope there are few who have so clear a sense of their obligations to him, who make such unsuitable and languid returns as I do. I think I have a desire to serve him better; but, alas! evil is present with me. Surely I shall feel something like shame and regret for my coldness, even in heaven;— for I find I am never happier than when I am most ashamed of myself upon this account here.

I am, &c.

LETTER XXVIII

The Blessedness of the Believer.

My Lord,

THE apostle speaks of a blessedness, which it is the design of the Gospel to impart to those who receive it. The Galatians once had it, and spoke of it. The apostle reminds them of their loss, which is left upon record as a warning to us. His expression has led me sometimes to consider wherein a Christian's present blessedness consists. I mean that which is attainable in this state of trial, and the sense and exercise of which may be, and

[1] Earth we must leave, and home and darling wife; nor of the trees thou tendest now, will any follow thee, its short-lived master, except the hated cypress.

too often is, suspended and taken from us. It is a blessedness which, if we speak of man in a natural state, his eye hath not seen, nor his ear heard so as to understand it, nor can the idea of it arise in his heart. It is no way dependent upon outward circumstances. Prosperity cannot impart it, preserve, or supply the want of it; nor can adversity put it out of our reach. The wise cannot acquire it by dint of superior abilities; nor shall the simple miss it for want of capacity.

The state of true believers, compared with that of others, is always blessed. If they are born from above, and united to Jesus, they are delivered from condemnation, and are heirs of eternal life, and may therefore well be accounted happy. But I consider now, not their harvest, but their first-fruits; not their portion in reversion, but the *earnest* attainable in this life; not what they *shall be* in heaven, but what, in an humble attendance upon the Lord, they *may be* while upon earth. There is even at present a prize of our high calling set before us. It is much to be desired, that we had such a sense of its value as might prompt us so to run that we might obtain. I have thought this blessedness may be comprised in five particulars, though, in order to take a succinct view of the subject, some of these might be branched out into several others; but I would not by too many subdivisions give my letter the air of a sermon.

In the first place, a clear, well-grounded, habitual persuasion of our acceptance in the Beloved is attainable; and though we may be safe, we cannot be said to enjoy blessedness without it. To be in a state of suspense and uncertainty in a point of so great importance, is painful; and the Lord has accordingly provided, that his people may have strong consolation on this head. They are blessed, therefore, who have such views of the power, grace, and suitableness of Jesus, and the certainty and security of redemption in him, together with such a consciousness that they have anchored their hopes, and ventured their all, upon his person, work, and promise, as furnishes them with a ready answer to all the cavils of unbelief and Satan, in the apostle's manner, Rom. viii. 31-37. That Paul could thus challenge and triumph over all charges and enemies, was not an appendage of his office as an apostle, but a part of his experience as a believer; and it lies equally open to us: for we have the same Gospel and the same promises as he had; nor is the efficacy of the Holy Spirit's teaching, a whit weakened by length of time. But many stop short of this. They have a hope, but it rather springs from their frames and feelings, than from a spiritual apprehension of the Redeemer's engagements and fulness, and therefore fluctuates and changes like the weather. Could they be persuaded to pray with earnestness and importunity, as the apostle prays for them, Ephes. i. 17, 18 and iii. 16-19 they would find a blessedness which they have not yet known; for it is said, "Ask, and ye shall receive."—And it is said likewise, "Ye receive not, because ye ask not."

Could this privilege be enjoyed singly, the natural man would have no objection to it. He would (as he thinks) be pleased to know he should be saved at last, provided that while here he might live in his sins. But the believer will not, cannot think himself blessed, unless he has likewise a conscience void of offence. This was the apostle's daily exercise, though no one was farther from a legal spirit, or more dependent upon Jesus for acceptance. But if we live in any known sin, or allow ourselves in the customary omission of any known duty, supposing it possible, in such a case, to preserve a sense of our acceptance (which can hardly be supposed, for if the Spirit be grieved, our evidences decline of course), yet we could not be easy. If a traveller was absolutely sure of reaching his journey's end in safety; yet if he walked with a thorn in his foot, he must take every step in pain. Such a thorn will be felt in the conscience, till we are favoured with a simplicity of heart, and made willing in all things, great or small, to yield obedience to the authority of the Lord's precepts, and make them the standing rule of our conduct, without wilfully admitting a single exception. At the best, we shall be conscious of innumerable shortcomings, and shameful defilement; but these things will not break our peace, if our hearts are upright. But if we trifle with light, and connive at what we know to be wrong, we shall be weak, restless, and uncomfortable. How many, who we would hope are the children of the King, are lean from day to day, because some right-hand or right-eye evil, which

they cannot persuade themselves to part with, keeps them halt-
ing between two opinions; and they are as distant from happiness, as they are from the possibility of reconciling the incompatible services of God and the world. But happy indeed is he
who condemneth not himself in that thing which he alloweth.

Real communion with the Lord, in his appointed means of
grace, is likewise an important branch of this blessedness. They
were instituted for this end, and are sufficient, by virtue of
his power and Spirit, to answer it. I do not believe this enjoy-
ment will be always equal. But I believe a comfortable sense of
it, in some measure, is generally attainable. To read the Scripture, not as an attorney may read a will, merely to know the
sense; but as the heir reads it, as a description and proof of
his interest: to hear the Gospel, as the voice of our Beloved,
so as to have little leisure either for admiring the abilities, or
censuring the defects of the preacher; and, in prayer, to feel a
liberty of pouring out our hearts before the Lord, to behold
some glances of his goodness passing before us, and to breathe
forth before him the tempers of a child, the spirit of adoption:
and thus, by beholding his glory, to be conformed more and
more to his image, and to renew our strength by drawing
water out of the wells of salvation—herein is blessedness. They
who have tasted it can say: " It is good for me to draw nigh to
God." The soul thus refreshed by the water of life, is preserved
from thirsting after the vanities of the world; thus instructed in
the sanctuary, comes down from the mount filled with heavenly
wisdom, anointed with a holy unction, and thereby qualified
to judge, speak, and act in character, in all the relations and
occasions of secular life. In this way, besides the pleasure,
a spiritual taste is acquired, something analogous to the meaning of the word taste when applied to music or good-breeding,
by which discords and improprieties are observed and avoided,
as it were by instinct, and what is right is felt and followed,
not so much by the force of rules, as by a habit insensibly
acquired, and in which the substance of all necessary rules is,
if I may so say, digested. O that I knew more of this blessedness, and more of its effects!

Another branch of blessedness, is a power of reposing ourselves and our concerns upon the Lord's faithfulness and care;

and may be considered in two respects: a reliance upon him
that he will surely provide for us, guide us, protect us, be our
help in trouble, our shield in danger; so that however poor,
weak, and defenceless in ourselves, we may rejoice in his all-
sufficiency as our own;—and further, in consequence of this, a
peaceful, humble submission to his will, under all events which,
upon their first impression, are contrary to our own views and
desires. Surely, in a world like this, where everything is uncertain, where we are exposed to trials on every hand, and
know not but a single hour may bring forth something painful, yea dreadful to our natural sensations, there can be no
blessedness, but so far as we are thus enabled to entrust and
resign all to the direction and faithfulness of the Lord our Shepherd. For want of more of this spirit, multitudes of professing
Christians perplex and wound themselves, and dishonour their
high calling, by continual anxieties, alarms, and complaints.
They think nothing safe under the Lord's keeping, unless their
own eye is likewise upon it; and are seldom satisfied with any
of his dispensations: for though he gratify their desires in
nine instances, a refusal in the tenth spoils the relish of all,
and they show the truths of the Gospel can afford them little
comfort, if self is crossed. But blessed is the man who trusteth
in the Lord, and whose hope the Lord is. He shall not be
afraid of evil tidings: he shall be kept in perfect peace, though
the earth be moved, and the mountains cast into the midst of
the sea.

The paper admonishes me it is time to relieve your lordship:
—and I have not room to detain you long upon the fifth particular. It belongs to a believer's blessedness, to feel his spirit
cheerful and active for the Lord's service in the world. For to
what other end should he wish to live? If he thought of himself only, it would be better to depart and be with Jesus immediately. But he is a debtor to his grace and love; and
though, strictly, he can make no returns,—yet he longs to
show his thankfulness: and if the Lord give him a heart to
redeem his time, to devote his strength and influence, and lay
himself out for his service,—that he may be instrumental in
promoting his cause, in comforting his people,—or enable him
to let his light shine before men, that his God and Father may

be honoured;—he will account it blessedness. This is indeed the great end of life, and he knows it will evidently appear so at the approach of death; and therefore, while others are cumbered about many things, he esteems this the one thing needful.

I remain, my lord, &c.

LETTER XXIX

The Character of a Christian.

My Lord,

WITHOUT any preamble, I purpose now to wait on your lordship, with a few thoughts on the meaning of that name which first obtained at Antioch, in other words, what it is to be a Christian? What are the effects, which (making allowance for the unavoidable infirmities attending upon the present state of mortality) may be expected from a real experimental knowledge of the Gospel? I would not insinuate that none are Christians who do not come up to the character I would describe; for then I fear I should unchristian myself: but only to consider what the Scripture encourages us to aim at as the prize of our high calling in this life. It is generally allowed and lamented, that we are too apt to live below our privileges, and to stop short of what the spirit and the promises of the Gospel point out to us as attainable.

Mr. Pope's admired line, " An honest man's the noblest work of God," may be admitted as a truth when rightly explained. A Christian is the noblest work of God in this visible world, and bears a much brighter impression of his glory and goodness than the sun in the firmament; and none but a Christian can be strictly and properly honest: all others are too much under the power of self to do universally to others as they would others should do unto them; and nothing but a uniform conduct upon this principle deserves the name of honesty.

The Christian is a new creature, born and taught from above.

He has been convinced of his guilt and misery as a sinner, has fled for refuge to the hope set before him, has seen the Son and believed on him: his natural prejudices against the glory and grace of God's salvation have been subdued and silenced by almighty power; he has accepted the Beloved, and is made acceptable in him: he now knows the Lord; has renounced the confused, distant, uncomfortable notions he once formed of God; and beholds him in Christ, who is the way, the truth, and the life, the only door by which we can enter to any true satisfying knowledge of God, or communion with him. But he sees God in Christ, reconciled, a Father, a Saviour, and a Friend, who has freely forgiven him all his sins, and given him the spirit of adoption: he is now no longer a servant, much less a stranger, but a son; and because a son, an heir already interested in all the promises, admitted to the throne of grace, and an assured expectant of eternal glory. The Gospel is designed to give us not only a peradventure or a probability, but a certainty both of our acceptance and our perseverance, till death shall be swallowed up in life. And though many are sadly fluctuating and perplexed upon this head, and perhaps all are so for a season; yet there are those who can say: "We know that we are of God," and therefore they are steadfast and unmoveable in his way; because they are confident that their labour shall not be in vain, but that when they shall be absent from the body, they shall be present with their Lord. This is the state of the advanced, experienced Christian, who, being enabled to make his profession the chief business of his life, is strong in the Lord, and in the power of his might. Everyone who has this hope in Christ, purifieth himself, even as he is pure. I would now attempt a sketch of the Christian's temper, formed upon these principles and hopes, under the leading branches of its exercise, respecting God, himself, and his fellow-creatures.

The Christian's temper God-ward is evidenced by *humility*. He has received from Gethsemane and Golgotha such a sense of the evil of sin, and of the holiness of God, combined with his matchless love to sinners, as has deeply penetrated his heart; he has an affecting remembrance of the state of rebellion and enmity in which he once lived against this holy and good God; and he has a quick perception of the defilements and defects

which still debase his best services. His mouth is therefore
stopped as to boasting; he is vile in his own eyes, and is filled
with wonder, that the Lord should visit such a sinner with such
a salvation. He sees so vast a disproportion between the obligations he is under to grace, and the returns he makes, that he
is disposed, yea constrained, to adopt the apostle's words without affectation, and to account himself less than the least of all
saints; and knowing his own *heart*, while he sees only the out-
side of others, he is not easily persuaded there can be a believer
upon earth so faint, so unfruitful, so unworthy as himself. Yet,
though abased, he is not discouraged, for he enjoys *peace*. The
dignity, offices, blood, righteousness, faithfulness, and compassion of the Redeemer, in whom he rests, trusts, and lives,
for wisdom, righteousness, sanctification, and redemption, are
adequate to all his wants and wishes, provide him with an
answer to every objection, and give him no less confidence in
God, than if he were sinless as an angel: for he sees, that though
sin has abounded in him, grace has much more abounded in
Jesus. With respect to the past, all things are become new;
with respect to the present and future, he leans upon an almighty
arm, and relies upon the word and power which made and
upholds the heavens and the earth. Though he feels himself
unworthy of the smallest mercies, he claims and expects the
greatest blessings that God can bestow; and being rooted and
grounded in the knowledge and love of Christ, his peace abides,
and is not greatly affected, either by the variation of his own
frames, or the changes of God's dispensations towards him
while here. With such a sense of himself, such a heart-felt
peace and heavenly hope, how can his spirit but breathe *love*
to his God and Saviour? It is indeed the perfection of his
character and happiness, that his soul is united by love to the
chief good. The love of Christ is the joy of his heart, and the
spring of his obedience. With his Saviour's presence, he finds
a heaven begun upon earth; and without it, all the other glories
of the heavenly state would not content him. The excellence
of Christ, his love to sinners, especially his dying love; his love
to himself in seeking and saving him when lost, saving him to
the uttermost—But I must stop! Your lordship can better
conceive than I can describe, how and why Jesus is dear to the

heart that knows him. That part of the Christian's life which is not employed in the active service of his Lord, is chiefly spent in seeking and maintaining communion with him. For this he plies the throne, and studies the word of grace, and frequents the ordinances, where the Lord has promised to meet with his people. These are his golden hours; and when thus employed, how poor and trivial does all that the world calls great and important appear in his eyes! Yea, he is solicitous to keep up an intercourse of heart with his Beloved in his busiest scenes; and so far as he can succeed, it alleviates all his labours, and sweetens all his troubles. And when he is neither communing with his Lord, nor acting for him, he accounts his time lost, and is ashamed and grieved. The truth of his love is manifested by *submission*. This is twofold, and absolute, and without reserve in each. He submits to his revealed will, as made known to him by precept, and by his own example. He aims to tread in his Saviour's footsteps, and makes conscience of *all* his commandments, without exception and without hesitation. Again, he submits to his providential will: he yields to his sovereignty, acquiesces in his wisdom; he knows he has no *right* to complain of anything, because he is a sinner; and he has no *reason*, because he is sure the Lord does all things well. Therefore his submission is not forced, but is an act of *trust*. He knows he is not more unworthy than he is unable to choose for himself, and therefore rejoices that the Lord has undertaken to manage for him; and were he compelled to make his own choice, he could only choose that all his concerns should remain in that hand to which he has already committed them. And thus he judges of *public* as well as of his personal affairs. He cannot be an unaffected spectator of national sins, nor without apprehension of their deserved consequences; he feels, and almost trembles for others, but he himself dwells under the shadow of the Almighty, in a sanctuary that cannot be forced; and therefore, should he see the earth shaken, and the mountains cast into the midst of the sea, his heart would not be greatly moved, for God is his refuge. The Lord reigns. He sees his Saviour's hand directing every dark appearance, and over-ruling all to the accomplishment of his own great purposes: this satisfies him; and though the winds

and waves should be high, he can venture his own little bark
in the storm, for he has an infallible and almighty Pilot on
board with him. And indeed, why should he fear when he has
nothing to lose? His best concerns are safe; and other things
he holds as gifts from his Lord, to whose call he is ready to
resign them, in whatever way he pleases, well knowing, that
creatures and instruments cannot of themselves touch a hair of
his head without the Lord's permission, and that if he does
permit them, it must be for the best.

I might enlarge further—But I shall proceed to consider
the Christian's temper respecting himself. He lives godly and
soberly. By sobriety we mean more than that he is not a
drunkard; his tempers toward God, of course, form him to a
moderation in all temporal things. He is not scrupulous or
superstitious; he understands the liberty of the Gospel, that
every creature of God is good if it be received with thanks-
giving: he does not aim at being needlessly singular, nor practise self-devised austerities. The Christian is neither a Stoic nor
a Cynic; yet he finds daily cause for watchfulness and restraint.
Satan will not often tempt a believer to gross crimes: our
greatest snares and sorest conflicts are usually found in things
lawful in themselves, but hurtful to us by their abuse, engross-
ing too much of our time, or of our hearts, or somehow indis-
posing us for communion with the Lord. The Christian will be
jealous of anything that might entangle his affections, damp
his zeal, or straiten him in his opportunities of serving his
Saviour. He is likewise content with his situation, because the
Lord chooses it for him; his spirit is not eager for additions and
alterations in his circumstances. If Divine Providence points
out and leads to a change, he is ready to follow, though it
should be what the world would call from a better to a worse;
for he is a pilgrim and a stranger here, and a citizen of heaven.
As people of fortune sometimes, in travelling, submit cheerfully
to inconvenient accommodations, very different from their
homes, and comfort themselves with thinking they are not
always to live so; so the Christian is not greatly solicitous about
externals. If he has them, he will use them moderately. If he
has but little of them, he can make a good shift without them:
he is but upon a journey, and will soon be at home. If he be

rich, experience confirms our Lord's words, Luke, xii. 15; and satisfies him, that a large room, a crowd of servants, and twenty dishes upon his table, add nothing to the real happiness of life. Therefore he will not have his heart set upon such things. If he be in a humbler state, he is more disposed to pity than to envy those above him; for he judges they must have many encumbrances from which he is freed. However, the will of God, and the light of his countenance, are the chief things the Christian, whether rich or poor, regards; and therefore his moderation is made known unto all men.

A third branch of the Christian's temper respects his fellow-creatures. And here, methinks, if I had not filled a sheet already, I could enlarge with pleasure. We have, in this degenerate day, among those who claim, and are allowed the name of Christian, too many of a narrow, selfish, mercenary spirit; but in the beginning it was not so. The Gospel is designed to cure such a spirit, but gives no indulgence to it. A Christian has the mind of Christ, who went about doing good, who makes his sun to shine upon the good and the evil, and sendeth rain on the just and the unjust. His Lord's example forms him to the habit of diffusive benevolence; he breathes a spirit of good-will to mankind, and rejoices in every opportunity of being useful to the souls and bodies of others, without respect to parties or interests. He commiserates, and would, if possible, alleviate, the miseries of all around him; and if his actual services are restrained by want of ability, yet all share in his sympathy and prayers. Acting in the spirit of his Master, he frequently meets with a measure of the like treatment; but if his good is requited with evil, he labours to overcome evil with good. He feels himself a sinner, and needs much forgiveness: this makes him ready to forgive. He is not haughty, captious, easily offended, or hard to be reconciled; for at the feet of Jesus he has learned meekness; and when he meets with unkindness or injustice, he considers, that, though he has not deserved such things from men, they are instruments employed by his heavenly Father (from whom he has deserved to suffer much more), for his humiliation and chastisement; and is therefore more concerned for their sins than for his own sufferings, and prays, after the pattern of his Saviour, "Father, forgive them, for they know not what they do!" He knows he is fallible; therefore cannot be positive. He knows he is frail; and therefore dares not be censorious. As a member of society, he is just, punctual in the discharge of every relative duty, faithful to his engagements and promises, rendering to all their dues, obedient to lawful authority, and acting to all men according to the golden rule, of doing as he would be done by. His conduct is simple, devoid of artifice, and consistent, attending to every branch of duty; and in the closet, the family, the church, and in the transactions of common life, he is the same man; for in every circumstance he serves the Lord, and aims to maintain a conscience void of offence in his sight. No small part of the beauty of his profession in the sight of men, consists in the due government of his tongue. The law of truth, and kindness, and purity, is upon his lips. He abhors lying; and is so far from inventing a slander, that he will not repeat a report to the disadvantage of his neighbour, however true, without a proper call. His converse is cheerful, but inoffensive; and he will no more wound another with his wit (if he has a talent that way), than with a knife. His speech is with grace, seasoned with salt, and suited to promote the peace and edification of all around him.

Such is the Christian in civil life; but though he loves all mankind, he stands in a nearer relation, and bears an especial brotherly love, to all who are partakers of the faith and hope of the Gospel. This regard is not confined within the pale of a denomination, but extended to all who love the Lord Jesus Christ in sincerity. He calls no man master himself; nor does he wish to impose a Shibboleth of his own upon others. He rejoices in the image of God, wherever he sees it, and in the work of God, wherever it is carried on. Though tenacious of the truths which the Lord has taught him, his heart is open to those who differ from him in less essential points, and allows to others that right of private judgement which he claims for himself, and is disposed to hold communion in love with all who hold the Head. He cannot indeed countenance those who set aside the one foundation which God has laid in Zion, and maintain errors derogatory to the honour of his Saviour, or subversive of the faith and experience of his people; yet he wishes well to their persons, pities and prays for them, and is ready in meekness to instruct them that oppose: but there is no bitterness in his zeal, being sensible that raillery and invective are dishonourable to the cause of truth, and quite unsuitable in the mouth of a sinner, who owes all that distinguishes him from the vilest of men to the free grace of God. In a word, he is influenced by the wisdom from above, which, as it is pure, is likewise peaceable, gentle, and easy to be entreated, full of mercy and good works, without partiality, and without hypocrisy.

I must just recur to my first head; and observe, that with this spirit and deportment, the Christian, while he is enabled to maintain a conscience void of offence towards God and man, is still sensible and mindful of indwelling sin: he has his eye more upon this rule than upon his attainments; and therefore finds and confesses, that in everything he comes exceedingly short, and that his best services are not only defective but defiled: he accounts himself an unprofitable servant, is abased in his own eyes, and derives all his hope and comfort, as well as his strength, from Jesus, whom he has known, received, and trusted, to whom he has committed his soul, in whom he rejoices, and worships God in the spirit, renouncing all confidence in the flesh, and esteeming all things as loss, for the excellency of the knowledge of Christ Jesus his Lord.

If I have lately been rather tardy in making my payments to your lordship, I have proportionably increased the quantity. It is high time I should now relieve your patience. I hope I long to be a Christian indeed; and I hope this hasty exemplification of my wishes will answer to your lordship's experience better than I fear it does to my own. May I beg a remembrance in your prayers, that he who has given me to will and desire, may work in me to be and to do according to his own good pleasure.

I am, &c.

LETTER XXX

Cases of Conscience.

My Lord,

MY London journey, which prevented my writing in October, made me amends by an opportunity of waiting upon your lordship in person. Such seasons are not only pleasant at the time, but afford me pleasure in the review. I could have wished the half hour we were together by ourselves prolonged to half a day. The subject your lordship was pleased to suggest has been often upon my mind; and glad should I be, were I able to offer you anything satisfactory upon it. There is no doubt but first religious impressions are usually mingled with much of a legal spirit; and that conscience at such a time is not only tender, but misinformed and scrupulous: and I believe, as your lordship intimated, that when the mind is more enlightened, and we feel a liberty from many fetters we had imposed upon ourselves, we are in danger of verging too far towards the other extreme. It seems to me that no one person can adjust the medium, and draw the line exactly for another. There are so many particulars in every situation, of which a stranger cannot be a competent judge, and the best human advices and models are mixed with such defects, that it is not *right* to expect others to be absolutely guided by our rules, nor is it *safe* for us implicitly to adopt the decisions or practices of others. But the Scripture undoubtedly furnishes sufficient and infallible rules for every person, however circumstanced; and the throne of grace is appointed for us to wait upon the Lord for the best exposition of his precepts. Thus David often prays to be led in the right way, in the path of judgement. By frequent prayer, and close acquaintance with the Scripture, and an habitual attention to the frame of our hearts, there is a certain delicacy of spiritual taste and discernment to be acquired, which renders a nice disposition concerning the nature and limits of the Adiaphora, as they are called, or how near we may go to the utmost bounds of what is right, without being wrong, quite unnecessary. Love is the clearest and most persuasive casuist; and when our love to the Lord is in lively exercise, and the rule of his word is in our eye, we seldom make great mistakes. And I believe the overdoings of a young convert, proceeding from an honest simplicity of heart, and a desire of pleasing the Lord, are more acceptable in his sight than a certain coolness of conduct, which frequently takes place afterward, when we are apt to look back with pity upon our former weakness, and secretly to applaud ourselves for our present greater attainments in knowledge, though perhaps (alas, that it should ever be so!) we may have lost as much in warmth as we have gained in light.

From the time we know the Lord, and are bound to him by the cords of love and gratitude, the two chief points we should have in our view, I apprehend, are, to maintain communion with him in our own souls, and to glorify him in the sight of men. Agreeable to these views, though the Scripture does not enumerate or decide *totidem verbis*, for or against many things which some plead for, and others condemn; yet it furnishes us with some general canons, which, if rightly applied, will perhaps go a good way towards settling the debate, at least to the satisfaction of those who would rather please God than man. Some of these canons I will just mark to your lordship: Rom. xii. 1, 2. 1 Cor. viii. 13 and x. 31. 2 Cor. vi. 17. Ephes. iv. 30. Ephes. v. 11, 15, 16. 1 Thes. v. 22. Ephes. vi. 18. to which I may add, as suitable to the present times, Isa. xxii. 12. Luke, xxi. 34. I apprehend the spirit of these and similar passages of Scripture (for it would be easy to adduce a larger number) will bring a Christian under such restrictions as follow.

To avoid and forbear, for his own sake, whatever has a tendency to damp and indispose his spirit in attendance upon the means of grace; for such things, if they be not condemned as sinful *per se*, if they be not absolutely unlawful, yea though they be, when duly regulated, lawful and right (for often our chief snares are entwined with our blessings); yet if they have a repeated and evident tendency to deaden our hearts to divine things, of which each person's experience must determine, there must be something in them, either in season, measure or circumstance, wrong to us; and let them promise what they will, they do but rob us of our gold to pay us with counters. For the light of God's countenance, and an open cheerfulness of spirit in walking with him in private, is our chief joy; and we must be already greatly hurt, if anything can be pursued, allowed, or rested in, as a tolerable substitute for it.

For the sake of the church, and the influence example may have upon his fellow Christians, the law of charity and prudence will often require a believer to abstain from such things, not because they are unlawful, but inexpedient. Thus the apostle, though strenuous for the *right* of his Christian liberty, would have abridged himself of the use, so as to eat no meat, rather than offend a weak brother, rather than mislead him to act against the present light of his conscience. Upon this principle, if I could, without hurt to myself, attend some public amusements, as a concert or oratorio, and return from thence with a warm heart to my closet (the possibility of which, in my own case, I greatly question); yet I should think it my duty to forbear, lest some weaker than myself should be encouraged by me to make the like experiment, though in their own minds they might fear it was wrong, and have no other reason to think it lawful but because I did it: in which case I should suspect, that though I received no harm, they would. And I have known and conversed with some who I fear have made shipwreck of their profession, who have dated their first decline from imitating others, whom they thought wiser and better than themselves, in such kind of compliances. And it seems that an obligation of this sort of self-denial rises and is strengthened in proportion to the weight and influence of our characters. Were I in private life, I do not know that I should think it sinful to kill a partridge or a hare; but, as a minister, I no more dare do it than I dare join in a drunken frolic, because I know it would give offence to some, and be pleaded for as a licence by others.

There is a duty, and a charity likewise, which we owe to the world at large, as well as a faithfulness to God and his grace, in our necessary converse among them. This seems to require, that though we should not be needlessly singular, yet, for their instruction, and for the honour of our Lord and Master, we should keep up a certain kind of singularity, and show ourselves called to be a separated people: that though the providence of God has given us callings and relations to fill up (in which we cannot be too exact), yet we are not of the world, but belong to another community, and act from other principles, by other rules, and to other ends, than the generality of those about us. I have observed, that the world will often leave professors in quiet possession of their notions and sentiments, and places of worship, provided they will not be too stiff in the matter of conformity with their more general customs and amusements. But I fear many of them have had their prejudices strengthened against our holy religion by such compliances, and have thought that if there were such joy and comfort to be found in the ways of God as they hear from our pulpits, professors would not, in such numbers, and so often, run amongst them to beg a relief from the burden of time hanging upon their hands. As our Lord Jesus is the great representative of his people in heaven, he does them the honour to continue a succession of them as his representatives upon earth. Happy are they who are favoured with most of the holy unction, and best enabled to manifest to all around them, by their spirit, tempers, and conversation, what is the proper design and genuine effect of his Gospel upon the hearts of sinners.

In our way of little life in the country, serious people often complain of the snares they meet with from worldly people, and yet they must mix with them to get a livelihood. I advise them, if they can, to do their business with the world as they do it in the rain. If their business calls them abroad, they will not leave it undone for fear of being a little wet; but then, when it is done, they presently seek shelter, and will not stand in the rain for pleasure: so providential and necessary calls of duty, that lead us into the world, will not hurt us, if we find the spirit of the world unpleasant, and are glad to retire from it, and keep out of it as much as our relative duties will permit. That which is our cross, is not so likely to be our snare; but if that spirit, which we should always watch and pray against, infects and assimilates our minds to itself, then we are sure to suffer loss, and act below the dignity of our profession.

The value of time is likewise to be taken into the account. It is a precious talent, and our Christian profession opens a wide field for the due improvement of it. Much of it has been already lost, and therefore we are exhorted to redeem it. I think many things which custom pleads for will be excluded from a suitableness to a Christian, for this one reason, that they are not consistent with the simplest notion of the redemption of time. It is generally said we need relaxation; I allow it in a sense: the Lord himself has provided it; and because our spirits are too weak to be always upon the wing in meditation and prayer, he has appointed to all men, from the king downwards, something to do in a secular way. The poor are to labour, the rich are not exempted from something equivalent. And when everything of this sort in each person's situation is properly attended to, I apprehend, if the heart be alive, and in a right state, spiritual concernments will present themselves, as affording the noblest, sweetest, and most interesting relaxation from the cares and business of life; as, on the other hand, that business will be the best relaxation and unbending of the mind from religious exercises; and, between the two, perhaps there ought to be but little mere leisure time. A life *in this sense,* divided between God and the world, is desirable, when one part of it is spent in retirement, seeking after and conversing with him whom our souls love; and the other part of it employed in active services, for the good of our family, friends, the church, and society, for his sake. Every hour which does not fall in with one or other of these views, I apprehend is lost time.

The day in which we live seems likewise to call for something of a peculiar spirit in the Lord's people. It is a day of abounding sin, and I fear a day of impending judgement. The world, as it was in the days of Noah and Lot, is secure. We are soon to have a day of apparent humiliation; but the just causes for it are not confined to one day, but will subsist and too probably increase every day. If I am not mistaken in the signs of the time, there never was, within the annals of the English history, a period in which the spirit and employment described, Ezek. ix. 4. could be more suitable than the present. The Lord calls for mourning and weeping, but the words of many are stout against him; new species of dissipation are invented almost daily, and the language of those who bear the greatest sway in what is called the polite circle, I mean the interpretative language of their hearts, is like that of the rebellious Jews, Jer. xliv. 16, 17, &c. " As for the word which thou hast spoken, we will not hearken unto thee at all." In short, things are coming to a point, and it seems to be almost putting to the vote whether the Lord or Baal be God. In this state of affairs, methinks, we cannot be too explicit in avowing our attachment to the Lord, nor too careful in avoiding an improper correspondence with those who are in confederacy against him. We know not how soon we may greatly need that mark of providential protection which is restrained to those who sigh and cry for our abominations. Upon the whole, it appears to me, that it is more honourable, comfortable, and safe (if we cannot exactly hit the golden mean), to be thought by some too scrupulous and precise, than actually to be found too compliant with those things which, if not absolutely contrary to a divine commandment, are hardly compatible with the genius of the Gospel, or conformable to the mind that was in Christ Jesus, which ought also to be in his people. The places and amusements which the world frequent and admire, where occasions and temptations to sin are cultivated, where the law of what is called good-breeding is the only law which may not be violated with impunity, where sinful passions are provoked and indulged, where the fear of God is so little known or regarded that those who do fear him must hold their tongues though they should hear his name blasphemed, can hardly be a Christian's voluntary chosen ground. Yet I fear these characters will apply to every kind of polite amusement or assembly in the kingdom.

As to family connections, I cannot think we are bound to break or slight them. But as believers and their friends often live as it were in two elements, there is a mutual awkwardness, which makes their interviews rather dry and tedious. But upon that account they are less frequent than they would otherwise be, which seems an advantage. Both sides keep up returns of civility and affection; but as they cannot unite in sentiment and leading inclination, they will not contrive to be very often together, except there is something considerable given up by one or the other; and I think Christians ought to be very cautious what concessions they make upon this account. But, as I said at the beginning, no general positive rules can be laid down.

I have simply given your lordship such thoughts as have occurred to me while writing, without study, and without coherence. I dare not be dogmatical; but I think what I have written is agreeable both to particular texts and to the general tenor of Scripture. I submit it to your judgement.

I am, &c.

LETTER XXXI.

How to meet the Assaults of Satan.

Madam,

THOUGH in general I think myself tolerably punctual when I can answer a letter in six or seven weeks after the receipt, yet I feel some pain for not having acknowledged yours sooner. A case like that which you have favoured me with an account of, deserved an immediate attention, and when I read it, I proposed writing within a post or two, and I can hardly allow any plea of business to be sufficient excuse for delaying it so long; but our times are in the Lord's hands: may he now enable me to send you what may prove a word in season.

Your exercises have been by no means singular, though they may appear so to yourself; because, in your retired situation, you have not (as you observe) had much opportunity of knowing the experience of other Christians; nor has the guilt with which your mind has been so greatly burdened been properly your own. It was a temptation forced upon you by the enemy, and he shall answer for it. Undoubtedly it is a mournful proof of the depravity of our nature, that there is that within us which renders us so easily susceptive of his suggestions; a proof of our extreme weakness, that after the clearest and most satisfying evidences of the truth, we are not able to hold fast our confidence, if the Lord permits Satan to sift and shake us. But I can assure you these changes are not uncommon. I have known persons, who, after walking with God comfortably in the main for forty years, have been at their wit's end from such assaults as you mention, and been brought to doubt, not only of the reality of their own hopes, but of the very ground and foundation upon which their hopes were built. Had you remained, as it seems you once were, attached to the vanities of a gay and dissipated life, or could you have been content with a form of godliness, destitute of the power, it is probable you would have remained a stranger to these troubles. Satan would have employed his arts in a different and less perceptible way, to have soothed you into a false peace, and prevented any thought or suspicion of danger from arising in your mind. But when he could no longer detain you in his bondage, or seduce you back again into the world, then of course he would change his method, and declare open war against you. A specimen of his power and malice you have experienced; and the Lord, whom you loved, because he first loved you, permitted it, not to gratify Satan, but for your benefit—to humble and prove you, to show you what is in your heart, and to do you good in the issue. These things, for the present, are not joyous but grievous; yet in the end they yield the peaceable fruits of righteousness. In the mean time his eye is upon you; he has appointed bounds both to the degree and the duration of the trial; and he does and will afford you such supports, that you shall not be tried beyond what you are enabled to bear. I doubt not but your conflicts and sorrows will in due time terminate in praise and victory, and be sanctified to your fuller establishment in the truth.

I greatly rejoice in the Lord's goodness to your dying parent. How wisely timed, and how exactly suited, was that affecting dispensation, to break the force of those suggestions with which the enemy was aiming to overwhelm your spirit! He could not stand against such an illustrious demonstrative attestation that the doctrines you had embraced were not cunningly devised fables. He could proceed no farther in that way; but he is fruitful in resources. His next attempt, of course, was to fix guilt upon your conscience, as if you had yourself formed and willingly entertained those thoughts, which, indeed, you suffered with extreme reluctance and pain. Here likewise I find he succeeded for a time; but he who broke the former snare, will deliver you from this likewise.

The dark and dishonourable thoughts of God, which I hinted at as belonging to a natural state, are very different from the thoughts of your heart concerning him. You do not conceive of him as a hard master, or think you could be more happy in the breach than in the observance of his precepts. You do not prefer the world to his favour, or think you can please him, and make amends for your sins by an obedience of your own. These, and such as these, are the thoughts of the natural heart; the very reverse of yours. One thought, however, I confess you have indulged, which is no less dishonourable to the Lord than uncomfortable to yourself. You say, " I dare not believe that God will not impute to me as sin, the admission of thoughts which my soul ever abhorred, and to which my will never consented." Nay, you fear lest they should not only be imputed, but unpardonable. But how can this be possible? Indeed I will not call it your *thought*, it is your *temptation*. You tell me you have children. Then you will easily feel a plain illustration, which just now occurs to me. Let me suppose a case which has sometimes happened: a child, three or four years of age we will say, while playing incautiously at a little distance from home, should be suddenly seized and carried away by a gipsy. Poor thing! how terrified, how distressed must it be! Methinks I hear its cries. The sight and violence of the stranger, the recollection of its dear parents, the loss of its pleasing home, the dread and uncertainty of what is yet to befall it! is it not a wonder that it does not die in agonies? But see, help is at hand: the gipsy is pursued, and the child recovered. Now, my dear madam, permit me to ask you, if this were your child, how would you receive it? Perhaps, when the first transports of your joy for its safety would permit you, you might gently chide it for leaving your door; but would you disinherit it? Would you disown it? Would you deliver it up again to the gipsy with your own hands, because it had suffered a violence which it could not withstand, *which it abhorred, and to which its will never consented?* And yet what is the tenderness of a mother, of ten thousand mothers, to that which our compassionate Saviour bears to every poor soul that has been enabled to flee to him for salvation! Let us be far from charging that to him, of which we think we are utterly incapable ourselves. Take courage, madam, resist the devil, and he will flee from you. If he were to tempt you to anything criminal, you would start at the thought, and renounce it with abhorrence. Do the same when he tempts you to question the Lord's compassion and goodness. But there he imposes upon us with a show of humility, and persuades us that we do well to oppose our unworthiness as a sufficient exception to the many express promises of the word. It is said, the blood of Jesus cleanseth from all sin; that all manner of sin shall be forgiven for his sake; that whoever cometh he will in no wise cast out; and that he is able to save to the uttermost. Believe his word, and Satan shall be found a liar. If the child had deliberately gone away with the gipsy, had preferred that wretched way of life, had refused to return, though frequently and tenderly invited home; perhaps a parent's love might, in time, be too weak to plead for the pardon of such continued obstinacy. But, indeed, in this manner we have dealt with the Lord; and yet, whenever we are willing to return, he is willing to receive us with open arms, and without an upbraiding word; Luke, xv. 20-22. Though our sins have been deep-dyed, like scarlet and crimson, enormous as mountains, and countless as the sands, the sum total is but, *Sin has abounded*; but where sin hath abounded, grace has much more abounded. After all, I know the Lord keeps the key of comfort in his own hands, yet he has commanded us to attempt comforting one another. I should rejoice to be his instrument of administering comfort to you. I shall hope to hear from you soon; and that you will then be able to inform me he has restored to you the joys of his salvation. But if not yet, wait for him, and you shall not wait in vain.

I am, &c.

LETTER XXXII

How to keep close to the Lord.

Dear Madam,

You would have me tell you what are the best means to be used by a young person, to prevent the world, with all its opening and ensnaring scenes, from drawing the heart aside from God. It is an important question; but I apprehend your own heart will tell you, that you are already possessed of all the information concerning it which you can well expect from me. I could only attempt to answer it from the Bible, which lies open to you likewise. If your heart is like mine, it must confess, that when it turns aside from God, it is seldom through ignorance of the proper means or motives which should have kept us near him, but rather from an evil principle within, which prevails against our better judgement, and renders us unfaithful to light already received.

I could offer you rules, cautions, and advices in abundance; for I find it comparatively easy to preach to others. But if you should further ask me, " How shall I effectually reduce them to practice?" I feel that I am so deficient, and so much at a loss in this matter *myself*, that I know not well what to say to *you*. Yet something must be said.

In the first place, then, I would observe, that though it be our bounden duty, and the highest privilege we can propose to ourselves, to have our hearts kept close to the Lord; yet we must not expect it absolutely or perfectly, much less all at once: we shall keep close to him, in proportion as we are solidly convinced of the infinite disparity between him and the things which would presume to stand in competition with him, and the folly, as well as ingratitude, of departing from him. But these points are only to be learned by experience, and by smarting under a series of painful disappointments in our expectations from creatures. Our judgements may be quickly satisfied that his favour is better than life, while yet it is in the power of a mere trifle to turn us aside. The Lord permits us to feel our weakness, that we may be sensible of it; for though we are ready in words to confess that we are weak, we do not so properly know it, till that secret, though unallowed, dependence we have upon some strength in ourselves, is brought to the trial, and fails us. To be humble, and, like a little child, afraid of taking a step alone, and so conscious of snares and dangers around us, as to cry to him continually to hold us up that we may be safe, is the sure, the infallible, the only secret of walking closely with him.

But how shall we attain this humble frame of spirit? It must be, as I said, from a real and sensible conviction of our weakness and vileness, which we cannot learn (at least I have not been able to learn it) merely from books or preachers. The providence of God concurs with his Holy Spirit in his merciful design of making us acquainted with ourselves. It is indeed a great mercy to be preserved from such declensions as might fall under the notice of our fellow-creatures; but when *they* can observe nothing of consequence to object to us, things may be far from right with us in the sight of him who judges not only actions, but the thoughts and first motions of the heart. And indeed could we for a season so cleave to God as to find little or nothing in ourselves to be ashamed of, we are such poor creatures, that we should presently grow vain and self-sufficient, and expose ourselves to the greatest danger of falling.

There are, however, means to be observed on our part; and though you know them, I will repeat the principal, because you desire me. The first is Prayer; and here, above all things, we should pray for humility. It may be called both the guard of all other graces, and the soil in which they grow. The second, Attention to the Scripture. Your question is directly answered in Psalm cxix. 9. The precepts are our rule and delight, the promises our strength and encouragement: the good recorded of the saints is proposed for our encouragement; their miscarriages are as land-marks set up to warn us of the rocks and shoals which lie in the way of our passage. The study of the whole scheme of Gospel-salvation, respecting the person, life, doctrine, death, and glory of our Redeemer, is appointed to form our souls to a spiritual and divine taste; and so far as this prevails and grows in us, the trifles that would draw us from the Lord, will lose their influence, and appear, divested of the glare with which they strike the senses, mere vanity and nothing. The third grand means is, Consideration or Recollection; a careful regard to those temptations and snares, to which, from our tempers, situations, or connections, we are more immediately exposed, and by which we have been formerly hindered. It may be well in the morning, ere we leave our chambers, to forecast, as far as we are able, the probable circumstances of the day before us. Yet the observance of this, as well as of every rule that can be offered, may dwindle into a mere form. However, I trust the Lord, who has given you a desire to live to him, will be your guard and teacher. There is none teacheth like him.

I am, &c.

LETTER XXXIII.

The Benefits of Affliction.

My dear Madam,

I HAVE often preached to others of the benefit of affliction; but my own path for many years has been so smooth, and my trials, though I have not been without trials, comparatively so light and few, that I have seemed to myself to speak by rote upon a subject of which I had not a proper feeling. Yet the many exercises of my poor afflicted people, and the sympathy the Lord has given me with them in their troubles, has made this a frequent and favourite topic of my ministry among them. The advantages of afflictions, when the Lord is pleased to employ them for the good of his people, are many and great. Permit me to mention a few of them; and the Lord grant that we may all find those blessed ends answered to ourselves, by the trials he is pleased to appoint us.

Afflictions quicken us to prayer. It is a pity it should be so; experience testifies that a long course of ease and prosperity, without painful changes, has an unhappy tendency to make us cold and formal in our secret worship; but troubles rouse our spirits, and constrain us to call upon the Lord in good earnest, when we feel a need of that help which we only can have from him.

They are useful, and in a degree necessary, to keep alive in us a conviction of the vanity and unsatisfying nature of the present world, and all its enjoyments; to remind us that this is not our rest, and to call our thoughts upwards, where our true treasure is, and where our conversation ought to be. When things go on much to our wish, our hearts are too prone to say, It is good to be here. It is probable, that had Moses, when he came to invite Israel to Canaan, found them in prosperity, as in the days of Joseph, they would have been very unwilling to remove; but the afflictions they were previously brought into made his message welcome. Thus the Lord, by pain, sickness, and disappointments, by breaking our cisterns and withering our gourds, weakens our attachment to this world, and makes the thought of quitting it more familiar and more desirable.

A child of God cannot but greatly desire a more enlarged and experimental acquaintance with his holy word; and this attainment is greatly promoted by our trials. The far greater part of the promises in Scripture are made and suited to a state of affliction; and, though we may believe they are true, we cannot so well know their sweetness, power, and suitableness, unless we ourselves are in a state to which they refer. The Lord says, " Call upon me in the day of trouble, and I will deliver."— Now till the day of trouble comes, such a promise is like a city of refuge to an Israelite, who not having slain a man, was in no danger of the avenger of blood. He had a privilege near him, of which he knew not the use and value, because he was not in the case for which it was provided. But some can say, " I not only believe this promise upon the authority of the speaker, but I can set my seal to it: I have been in trouble; I took this course for relief, and I was not disappointed. The Lord verily heard and delivered me." Thus afflictions likewise give occasion of our knowing and noticing more of the Lord's wisdom, power, and goodness, in supporting and relieving, than we should otherwise have known.

I have not time to take another sheet, and must therefore contract my homily. Afflictions evidence to ourselves, and manifest to others, the reality of grace. And when we suffer as Christians, exercise some measure of that patience and submission, and receive some measure of these supports and supplies, which the Gospel requires and promises to believers, we are more confirmed that we have not taken up with mere notions; and others may be convinced that we do not follow cunningly devised fables. They likewise strengthen by exercise our graces: as our limbs and natural powers would be feeble if not called to daily exertion; so the graces of the Spirit would languish, without something provided to draw them out to use. And, to say no more, they are honourable, as they advance our conformity to Jesus our Lord, who was a man of sorrows for our sake. Methinks, if we might go to heaven without suffering, we should be unwilling to desire it. Why should we ever wish to go by any other path than that which he has consecrated and endeared by his own example? especially as his people's sufferings are not penal; there is no wrath in them; the cup he puts in their hands is very different from that which he drank for their sakes, and is only medicinal to promote their chief good. Here I must stop; but the subject is fruitful, and might be pursued through a quire of paper.

I am, &c.

LETTER XXXIV

Contrary Principles in the Believer.

My dear Madam,

WHAT can I say for myself, to let your obliging letter remain so long unanswered, when your kind solicitude for us induced you to write? I am ashamed of the delay. You would have heard from me immediately, had I been at home. But I have reason to be thankful that we were providentially called to London a few days before the fire; so that Mrs. **** was mercifully preserved from the alarm and shock she must have felt, had she been upon the spot. Your letter followed me hither, and was in my possession more than a week before my return. I purposed writing every day, but indeed I was much hurried and engaged. Yet I am not excused: I ought to have saved time from my meals and my sleep, rather than appear negligent or ungrateful. I now seize the first post I could write by since I came home. The fire devoured twelve houses; and it was a mercy, and almost a miracle, that the whole town was not destroyed; which must, humanly speaking, have been the case, had not the night been calm, as two thirds of the buildings were thatched. No lives were lost; no person considerably hurt; and I believe the contributions of the benevolent will prevent the loss from being greatly felt. It was at the distance of a quarter of a mile from my house.

Your command limits my attention, at present, to a part of your letter, and points me out a subject. Yet at the same time you lay me under a difficulty. I would not willingly offend you, and I hope the Lord has taught me not to aim at saying handsome things. I deal not in compliments, and religious compliments are the most unseemly of any. But why might I not express my sense of the grace of God, manifested in you as well as in another? I believe our hearts are all alike, destitute of every good, and prone to every evil. Like money from the same mint, they bear the same impression of total depravity: but grace makes a difference, and grace deserves the praise. Perhaps it ought not greatly to displease you, that others do, and must, and will think better of you than you do of yourself. If I do, how can I help it, when I form my judgement entirely from what you say and write? I cannot consent that you should seriously appoint me to examine and judge of your state. I thought you knew, beyond the shadow of a doubt, what your views and desires are; yea, you express them in your letter, in full agreement with what the Scripture declares of the principles, desires, and feelings of a Christian. It is true that you feel contrary principles, that you are conscious of defects and defilements; but it is equally true, that you could not be right if you did not feel these things. To be conscious of them, and humbled for them, is one of the surest marks of grace; and to be more deeply sensible of them than formerly, is the best evidence of growth in grace. But when the enemy would tempt us to doubt and distrust, because we are not perfect, then he fights, not only against our peace, but against the honour and faithfulness of our dear Lord. Our righteousness is in him, and our hope depends, not upon the exercise of grace in us, but upon the fulness of grace and love in him, and upon his obedience unto death.

There is, my dear madam, a difference between the holiness of a sinner and that of an angel. The angels have never sinned, nor have they tasted of redeeming love; they have no inward conflicts, no law of sin warring in their members: their obedience is perfect; their happiness is complete. Yet if I be found among redeemed sinners, I need not wish to be an angel. Perhaps God is not less glorified by your obedience, and not to shock you, I will add by mine, than by Gabriel's. It is a mighty manifestation of his grace indeed, when it can live, and act, and conquer in such hearts as ours; when, in defiance of an evil nature and an evil world, and all the force and subtilty of Satan, a weak worm is still upheld, and enabled not only to climb, but to thresh the mountains; when a small spark is preserved through storms and floods. In these circumstances, the work of grace is to be estimated, not merely from its imperfect appearance, but from the difficulties it has to struggle with and overcome; and therefore our holiness does not consist in great attainments, but in spiritual desires, in hungerings, thirstings, and mournings; in humiliation of heart, poverty of spirit, submission, meekness; in cordial admiring thoughts of Jesus, and dependence upon him alone for all we want. Indeed these may be said to be great attainments; but they who have most of them are most sensible that they, in and of themselves, are nothing, have nothing, can do nothing, and see daily cause for abhorring themselves, and repenting in dust and ashes.

Our view of death will not always be alike, but in proportion to the degree in which the Holy Spirit is pleased to communicate his sensible influence. We may anticipate the moment of dissolution with pleasure and desire in the morning, and be ready to shrink from the thought of it before night. But though our frames and perceptions vary, the report of faith concerning it is the same. The Lord usually reserves dying strength for a dying hour. When Israel was to pass Jordan, the Ark was in the river; and though the rear of the host could not see it, yet as they successively came forward and approached the banks, they all beheld the Ark, and all went safely over. As you are not weary of living, if it be the Lord's pleasure, so I hope, for the sake of your friends and the people whom you love, he will spare you amongst us a little longer; but when the time shall arrive which he has appointed for your dismission, I make no doubt but he will overpower all your fears, silence all your enemies, and give you a comfortable, triumphant entrance into his kingdom. You have nothing to fear from death; for Jesus, by dying, has disarmed it of its sting, has perfumed the grave, and opened the gates of glory for his believing people. Satan, so far as he is permitted, will assault our peace, but he is a vanquished enemy: our Lord holds him in a chain, and sets him bounds which he cannot pass. He provides for us likewise the whole armour of God and has promised to cover our heads himself in the day of battle, to bring us honourably through every skirmish, and to make us more than conquerors at last. If you think my short unexpected interview with Mr. C**** may justify my wishing he should know that I respect his character, love his person, and rejoice in what the Lord has done and is doing for him and by him, I beg you to tell him so: but I leave it entirely to you.

We join in most affectionate respects.

I am, &c.

LETTER XXXV

Christ All-sufficient.

YOU see I am mindful of my promise, and glad should I be to write something that the Lord may be pleased to make a word in season. I went yesterday into the pulpit very dry and heart-less. I seemed to have fixed upon a text, but when I came to the pinch, it was so shut up that I could not preach from it. I had hardly a minute to choose, and therefore was forced to snatch at that which came first upon my mind, which proved 2 Tim. i. 12. Thus I set off at a venture, having no resource but in the Lord's mercy and faithfulness; and indeed what other can we wish for? Presently my subject opened, and I know not when I have been favoured with more liberty. Why do I tell you this? Only as an instance of his goodness, to encourage you to put your strength in him, and not to be afraid, even when you feel your own weakness and insufficiency most sen-sibly. We are never more safe, never have more reason to ex-pect the Lord's help, than when we are most sensible that we can do nothing without him. This was the lesson Paul learnt, to rejoice in his own poverty and emptiness, that the power of Christ might rest upon him. Could Paul have done anything, Jesus would not have had the honour of doing all. This way of being saved entirely by grace, from first to last, is contrary to our natural wills: it mortifies self, leaving it nothing to boast of, and through the remains of an unbelieving legal spirit, it often seems discouraging. When we think ourselves so utterly helpless and worthless, we are too ready to fear that the Lord will therefore reject us; whereas, in truth, such a poverty of spirit is the best mark we can have of an interest in his promises and care.

How often have I longed to be an instrument of establishing you in the peace and hope of the Gospel, and I have but one way of attempting it, by telling you over and over of the power and grace of Jesus. You want nothing to make you happy, but to have the eyes of your understanding more fixed upon the Redeemer, and more enlightened by the Holy Spirit to behold his glory. O he is a suitable Saviour! he has power, authority, and compassion to save to the uttermost. He has given his word of promise to engage our confidence, and he is able and faithful to make good the expectations and desires he has raised in us. Put your trust in him; believe (as we say) through thick and thin, in defiance of all objections from within and without. For this, Abraham is recommended as a pattern to us. He overlooked all difficulties; he ventured and hoped even against hope, in a case which, to appearance, was desperate; because he knew that he who had promised was also able to perform.

Your sister is much upon my mind. Her illness grieves me; were it in my power, I would quickly remove it: the Lord can, and I hope will, when it has answered the end for which he sent it. I trust he has brought her to us for good, and that she is chastised by him that she may not be condemned with the world. I hope, though she says little, she lifts up her heart to him for a blessing. I wish you may be enabled to leave her, and yourself, and all your concerns, in his hands. He has a sovereign right to do with us as he pleases; and if we consider what we are, surely we shall confess we have no reason to complain: and to those who seek him, his sovereignty is exercised in a way of grace. All shall work together for good: everything is needful that he sends; nothing can be needful that he withholds. Be content to bear the cross; others have borne it before you. You have need of patience; and if you ask, the Lord will give it: but there can be no settled peace till our will is in a measure subdued. Hide yourself under the shadow of his wings; rely upon his care and power; look upon him as a physician who has graciously undertaken to heal your soul of the worst of sicknesses, sin. Yield to his prescriptions, and fight against every thought that would represent it as desirable to be permitted to choose for yourself. When you cannot see your way, be satisfied that he is your leader. When your spirit is overwhelmed within you, he knows your path: he will not leave you to sink. He has appointed seasons of refreshment, and you shall find he does not forget you. Above all, keep close to the throne of grace. If we seem to get no good by attempting to draw near him, we may be sure we shall get none by keeping away from him.

I am, &c.

LETTER XXXVI

Blessed are they that Mourn.

My Dear Madam,

THE complaints you make are inseparable from a spiritual acquaintance with our own hearts: I would not wish you to be less affected with a sense of indwelling sin. It becomes us to be humbled into the dust; yet our grief, though it cannot be too great, may be under a wrong direction; and if it leads us to impatience or distrust, it certainly is so.

Sin is the sickness of the soul, in itself mortal and incurable as to any power in heaven or earth but that of the Lord Jesus only. But he is the great, the infallible physician. Have we the privilege to know his name? Have we been enabled to put ourselves into his hand? We have then no more to do but to attend his prescriptions, to be satisfied with his methods, and to wait his time. It is lawful to wish we were well; it is natural to groan, being burdened; but still he must and will take his own course with us; and, however dissatisfied with ourselves, we ought still to be thankful that he has begun his work in us, and to believe that he will also make an end. Therefore while we mourn, we should likewise rejoice; we should encourage ourselves to expect all that he has promised; and we should limit our expectations by his promises. We are sure, that when the Lord delivers us from the guilt and dominion of sin, he could with equal ease free us entirely from sin, if he pleased. The doctrine of sinless perfection is not to be rejected, as though it were a thing simply impossible in itself, for nothing is too hard for the Lord, but because it is contrary to that method which he has chosen to proceed by. He has appointed that sanctification should be effected, and sin mortified, not at once completely, but by little and little; and doubtless he has wise reasons for it. Therefore, though we are to desire a growth in grace, we should, at the same time, acquiesce in his appointment, and not be discouraged or despond, because we feel that conflict which his word informs us will only terminate with our lives.

Again, some of the first prayers which the Spirit of God teaches us to put up, are for a clearer sense of the sinfulness of sin, and our vileness on account of it. Now, if the Lord is pleased to answer your prayers in this respect, though it will afford you cause enough for humiliation, yet it should be received likewise with thankfulness, as a token for good. Your heart is not worse than it was formerly, only your spiritual knowledge is increased; and this is no small part of the growth in grace which you are thirsting after, to be truly humbled, and emptied, and made little in your own eyes.

Further, the examples of the saints recorded in Scripture prove (and indeed of the saints in general), that the greater measure any person has of the grace of God in truth, the more conscientious and lively they have been. And the more they have been favoured with assurances of the Divine favour, so much the more deep and sensible their perception of indwelling sin and infirmity has always been. So it was with Job, Isaiah, Daniel, and Paul. It is likewise common to overcharge ourselves. Indeed we cannot think ourselves worse than we really are; yet some things which abate the comfort and alacrity of our Christian profession are rather impediments than properly sinful, and will not be imputed to us by him who knows our frame, and remembers that we are but dust. Thus, to have an infirm memory, to be subject to disordered, irregular, or low spirits, are faults of the constitution, in which the *will* has no share, though they are all burdensome and oppressive, and sometimes needlessly so, by our charging ourselves with guilt on their account. The same may be observed of the unspeakable and fierce suggestions of Satan, with which some persons are pestered, but which shall be laid to him from whom they proceed, and not to them who are troubled and terrified because they are forced to feel them. *Lastly*, It is by the experience of these evils within ourselves, and by feeling our utter insufficiency, either to perform duty or to withstand our enemies, that the Lord takes occasion to show us the suitableness, the sufficiency, the freeness, the unchangeableness of his power and grace. This is the inference St. Paul draws from his complaints, Rom. vii. 25, and he learnt it upon a trying occasion from the Lord's own mouth, 2 Cor. xii. 8, 9.

Let us then, dear madam, be thankful and cheerful, and while we take shame to ourselves, let us glorify God by giving Jesus the honour due to his name. Though we are poor, he is rich; though we are weak, he is strong; though we have nothing, he possesses all things. He suffered for us; he calls us to be conformed to him in sufferings. He conquered in his own person, and he will make each of his members more than conquerors in due season. It is good to have one eye upon ourselves, but the other should ever be fixed on him who stands in the relation of Saviour, Husband, Head, and Shepherd. In him we have righteousness, peace, and power. He can control all that we fear; so that if our path should be through the fire or through the water, neither the flood shall drown us, nor the flame kindle upon us, and ere long he will cut short our conflicts, and say, Come up hither. " Then shall our grateful songs abound, and every tear be wiped away." Having such promises and assurances, let us lift up our banner in his name, and press on through every discouragement.

With regard to company that have not a savour of the best things, as it is not your choice, I would advise you (when necessary) to bear it as a cross: we cannot suffer by being where we ought to be, except through our own impatience; and I have an idea, that when we are providentially called amongst such (for something is due to friends and relations, whether they walk with us or no), that the hours need not be wholly lost: nothing can pass but may be improved; the most trivial conversation may afford us new views of the heart, new confirmation of Scripture, and renew a sense of our obligations to distinguishing grace, which has made us in any degree to differ.

I would wish when you go amongst your friends, that you do not confine your views to getting safe away from them without loss, but entertain a hope that you may be sent to do some of them good. You cannot tell what effect a word or a look may have, if the Lord is pleased to bless it. I think we may humbly hope, that while we sincerely desire to please the Lord, and to be guided by him in all things, he will not suffer us to take a journey, or hardly to make a short visit, which shall not answer some good purpose to ourselves or others, or both. While your gay friends affect an air of raillery, the Lord may give you a secret witness in their consciences; and something they observe in you, or hear from you, may set them on thinking perhaps after you are gone, or after the first occasion has entirely slipped your memory; Eccles. xi. 1. For my own part, when I consider the power, the freedom of divine grace, and how sovereign the Lord is in the choice of the instruments and means by which he is pleased to work, I live in hopes from day to day of hearing of wonders of this sort. I despair of nobody: and if I sometimes am ready to think such or such a person seems more unlikely than others to be brought in, I relieve myself by a possibility that that very person, and for that very reason, may be the first instance. The Lord's thoughts are not like ours: in his love and in his ways there are heights which we cannot reach, depths which we cannot fathom, lengths and breadths beyond the ken of our feeble sight. Let us then simply depend upon him, and do our little best, leaving the event in his hand.

I cannot tell if you know anything of Mrs. ****. In a letter I received yesterday she writes thus:— "I am at present very ill with some disorder in my throat, which seems to threaten my life; but death or life, things present or things to come, all things are mine, and I am Christ's, and Christ is God's. O glorious privilege! precious foundation of soul-rest and peace, when all things about us are most troublous! Soon we shall be at home with Christ, where sin, sorrow, and death have no place; and in the meantime our Beloved will lead us through the wilderness. How safe, how joyous are we, may we be, in the most evil case!"—If these should be some of the last notes of this swan, I think them worth preserving. May we not with good reason say, Who would not be a Christian? The Lord grant that you and I, madam, and yours and mine, may be happy in the same assurance, when we shall have death and eternity near in view.

I am, &c.

LETTER XXXVII

Conflict Exercises the Graces.

SINCE I wrote last, the Lord has been gracious to us here. He crowned the last year with his goodness, and renews his benefits to us every day. He has been pleased to bless the preaching of his Gospel amongst us, both to consolation and conviction; and several are, I hope, earnestly seeking him, who were lately dead in trespasses and sins. Dear Mr. **** was released from all his complaints the 25th of November. A few days before his death he was enabled to speak more intelligibly than usual for about a quarter of an hour, and expressed a comfortable hope, which was a great satisfaction to us; for though we had not the least doubt of his being built upon the rock, it was to us an answer to prayer that he could again speak the language of faith: and much prayer had been made on this account, especially that very evening. After that night he spoke little, and hardly took any notice, but continued chiefly drowsy till he died. I preached his funeral sermon from Lam. iii. 31, 32, 33. Mrs. L****'s complaint grows worse and worse; she suffers much in her body, and has much more perhaps to suffer; but her consolations in the Lord abound. He enables her to maintain faith, patience, and submission, in an exemplary manner, and shows us, in his dealings with her, that he is all-sufficient and faithful to those who put their trust in him. I am glad to hear that you had comfortable seasons while at Bath. It is indeed a great mercy that God's ordinances are established in that place of dissipation; and I hope many who go there with no higher view than to drink the Bath waters, will be brought to draw with joy the waters of life from those wells of salvation. He does nothing in vain, and when he affords the means, we may confidently hope he will bestow the blessing. The dissipation of spirit you complain of, when you are in a strange place, is I suppose felt by most, if not by all, who can be satisfied in no place without some token of the Lord's presence. I consider it rather as an infirmity than a sin, strictly speaking; though all our infirmities are sinful, being the effects of a depraved nature. In our present circumstances new things excite new ideas, and when our usual course of life is broken in upon, it disjoints and unsettles our thoughts. It is a proof of our weakness: it may and ought to be lamented; but I believe we shall not get the better of it, till we leave the mortal body to moulder into dust. Perhaps few suffer more inconvenience from this article than myself; which is one reason why I love home, and seldom leave it without some reluctance: and it is one reason why we should love heaven, and long for the hour when, at liberty from all encumbrance, we shall see the Lord without a vail, and serve him without distraction. The Lord, by his providence, seconds and confirms the declarations of his word and ministry. Much we read and much we hear concerning the emptiness, vanity, and uncertainty of the present state. When our minds are enlightened by his Holy Spirit, we receive and acknowledge what his word declares to be truth: yet if we remain long without changes, and our path is very smooth, we are for the most part but faintly affected with what we profess to believe. But when some of our dearest friends are taken from us, the lives of others threatened, and we ourselves are brought low with pain and sickness, then we not only *say* but *feel* that this must not, cannot be our rest. You have had several exercises of this kind of late in your family, and I trust you will be able to set your seal to that gracious word, That though afflictions in themselves are not joyous, but grievous, yet in due season they yield the peaceful fruits of righteousness. Various and blessed are the fruits they produce. By affliction prayer is quickened, for our prayers are very apt to grow languid and formal in a time of ease. Affliction greatly helps us to understand the Scriptures, especially the promises;

most of which being made to times of trouble, we cannot so
well know their fulness, sweetness, and certainty, as when we
have been in the situation to which they are suited, have been
enabled to trust and plead them, and found them fulfilled in
our own case. We are usually indebted to affliction as the
means or occasion of the most signal discoveries we are favoured
with of the wisdom, power, and faithfulness of the Lord.
These are best observed by the evident proofs we have that he
is near to support us under trouble, and that he can and does
deliver us out of it. Israel would not have seen so much of
the Lord's arm outstretched in their behalf, had not Pharaoh
oppressed, opposed, and pursued them. Afflictions are designed
likewise for the manifestation of our sincerity to ourselves and
to others. When faith endures the fire, we know it to be of the
right kind; and others, who see we are brought safe out, and
lose nothing but the dross, will confess that God is with us of
a truth, Dan. iii. 27, 28. Surely this thought should reconcile
us to suffer, not only with patience but with cheerfulness, if
God may be glorified in us. This made the apostle rejoice in
tribulation, that the power of Christ might be noticed, as resting upon him and working mightily in him. Many of our
graces likewise cannot thrive or show themselves to advantage
without trials; such as resignation, patience, meekness, long-
suffering. I observe some of the London porters do not appear
to be very strong men; yet they will trudge along under a burden which some stouter people could not carry so well: the
reason is, that they are accustomed to carry burdens, and by
continual exercise their shoulders acquire a strength suited to
their work. It is so in the Christian life; activity and strength
of grace is not ordinarily acquired by those who sit still and
live at ease, but by those who frequently meet with something
which requires a full exertion of what power the Lord has given
them. So again, it is by our own sufferings we learn to pity
and sympathize with others in their sufferings: such a compassionate disposition, which excites our feelings for the afflicted, is an eminent branch of the mind which was in Christ.
But these feelings would be very faint, if we did not in our experience know what sorrows and temptations mean. Afflictions
do us good likewise, as they make us more acquainted with

what is in our own hearts, and thereby promote humiliation and self-abasement. There are abominations which, like nests of vipers, lie so quietly within, that we hardly suspect they are there till the rod of affliction rouses them; then they hiss and show their venom. This discovery is indeed very distressing; yet, till it is made, we are prone to think ourselves much less vile than we really are, and cannot so heartily abhor ourselves and repent in dust and ashes.

But I must write a sermon rather than a letter, if I would enumerate all the good fruits which, by the power of sanctifying grace, are produced from this bitter tree. May we, under our several trials, find them all revealed in ourselves, that we may not complain of having suffered in vain. While we have such a depraved nature, and live in such a polluted world; while the roots of pride, vanity, self-dependence, self-seeking, are so strong within us, we need a variety of sharp dispensations to keep us from forgetting ourselves, and from cleaving to the dust.

I am, &c.

LETTER XXXVIII

Submission to the Will of the Lord.

IT is indeed natural to us to wish and to plan, and it is merciful in the Lord to disappoint our plans and to cross our wishes. For we cannot be safe, much less happy, but in proportion as we are weaned from our own wills, and made simply desirous of being directed by his guidance. This truth (when we are enlightened by his word) is sufficiently familiar to the judgement; but we seldom learn to reduce it into practice, without being trained awhile in the school of disappointment. The schemes we form look so plausible and convenient, that when they are broken we are ready to say, What a pity! We try again, and with no better success: we are grieved, and perhaps angry, and plan out another, and so on: at length, in a course of time, experience and observation begin to convince us, that we are not more able than we are worthy to choose aright for ourselves. Then the Lord's invitation to cast our cares upon him, and his promise to take care of us, appear valuable; and when *we* have done planning, *his* plan in our favour gradually opens, and he does more and better for us than we could either ask or think. I can hardly recollect a single plan of mine, of which I have not since seen reason to be satisfied, that had it taken place in season and circumstance just as I proposed, it would, humanly speaking, have proved my ruin; or, at least, it would have deprived me of the greater good the Lord had designed for me. We judge of things by their present appearances, but the Lord sees them in their consequences; if we could do so likewise, we should be perfectly of his mind; but as we cannot, it is an unspeakable mercy that he will manage for us, whether we are pleased with his management or not; and it is spoken of as one of his heaviest judgements, when he gives any person or people up to the way of their own hearts, and to walk after their own counsels.

Indeed, we may admire his patience towards us. If we were blind, and reduced to desire a person to lead us, and should yet pretend to dispute with him, and direct him at every step, we should probably soon weary him, and provoke him to leave us to find the way by ourselves if we could. But our gracious Lord is long-suffering and full of compassion; he bears with our frowardness, yet he will take methods both to shame and to humble us, and to bring us to a confession that he is wiser than we. The great and unexpected benefit he intends us, by all the discipline we meet with, is to tread down our wills, and bring them into subjection to his. So far as we attain to this, we are out of the reach of disappointment; for when the will of God can please us, we shall be pleased every day, and from morning to night; I mean with respect to his dispensations. O the happiness of such a life! I have an idea of it; I hope I am aiming at it, but surely I have not attained it. Self is active in my heart, if it does not absolutely reign there. I profess to believe that one thing is needful and sufficient, and yet my thoughts are prone to wander after a hundred more. If it be true, that the light of his countenance is better than life,

why am I solicitous about anything else? If he be all-sufficient, and gives me liberty to call him *mine,* why do I go a-
begging to creatures for help? If he be about my path and
bed; if the smallest, as well as the greatest events in which I
am concerned are under his immediate direction; if the very
hairs of my head are numbered; then my care (any farther
than a care to walk in the paths of his precepts, and to follow
the openings of his providence) must be useless and needless,
yea indeed sinful and heathenish, burdensome to myself, and
dishonourable to my profession. Let us cast down the load
we are unable to carry, and if the Lord be our shepherd, refer
all, and trust all to him. Let us endeavour to live to him and
for him to-day, and be glad that to-morrow, with all that is
behind it, is in his hands.

It is storied of Pompey, that when his friends would have
dissuaded him from putting to sea in a storm, he answered, " It
is necessary for me to sail, but it is not necessary for me to
live." O pompous speech, in Pompey's sense! He was full of
the idea of his own importance, and would rather have died
than have taken a step beneath his supposed dignity. But it
may be accommodated with propriety to a believer's case. It
becomes us to say, It is not necessary for me to be rich, or
what the world accounts wise; to be healthy, or admired by my
fellow-worms; to pass through life in a state of prosperity and
outward comfort; these things may be, or they may be otherwise, as the Lord in his wisdom shall appoint: but it is necessary for me to be humble and spiritual, to seek communion
with God, to adorn my profession of the Gospel, and to yield
submissively to his disposal, in whatever way, whether of
service or suffering, he shall be pleased to call me to glorify
him in the world. It is not necessary for me to live long,
but highly expedient that whilst I do live I should live to
him. Here then I would bound my desires; and here, having
his word both for my rule and my warrant, I am secured from
asking amiss. Let me have his presence and his Spirit, wisdom
to know my calling, and opportunities and faithfulness to improve them; and as to the rest, Lord, help me to say, What
thou wilt, when thou wilt, and how thou wilt.

I am, &c.

LETTER XXXIX

The Vanity of the World.

Dear Madam,

WHAT a poor, uncertain, dying world is this! What a wilderness in itself! How dark, how desolate, without the light of the Gospel and knowledge of Jesus! It does not appear so to us in a state of nature, because we are then in a state of enchantment, the magical lantern blinding us with a splendid delusion.

> Thus in the desert's dreary waste,
> By magic pow'r produc'd in haste,
>   As old romances say,
> Castles and groves, and music sweet,
> The senses of the trav'ller cheat,
>   And stop him in his way;
> But while he gazes with surprise,
> The charm dissolves, the vision dies;
>   'Twas but enchanted ground:
> Thus, if the Lord our spirit touch,
> The world, which promis'd us so much,
>   A wilderness is found.

It is a great mercy to be undeceived in time; and though our gay dreams are at an end, and we awake to everything that is disgustful and dismaying, yet we see a highway through the wilderness, a powerful guard, an infallible guide at hand to conduct us through; and we can discern, beyond the limits of the wilderness, a better land, where we shall be at rest and at home. What will the difficulties we met by the way then signify? The remembrance of them will only remain to heighten our sense of the love, care, and power of our Saviour and leader. O how shall we then admire, adore, and praise him, when he shall condescend to unfold to us the beauty, propriety, and harmony of the whole train of his dispensations towards us, and give us a clear retrospect of all the way and all the turns of our pilgrimage!

In the meanwhile, the best method of adorning our profession, and of enjoying peace in our souls, is simply to trust him, and absolutely to commit ourselves and our all to his management. By casting our burdens upon him, our spirits become light and cheerful; we are freed from a thousand anxieties and inquietudes, which are wearisome to our minds, and which with respect to events, are *needless* for us, yea, *useless*. But though it may be easy to speak of this trust, and it appears to our judgement perfectly right and reasonable, the actual attainment is a great thing; and especially so to trust the Lord, not by fits and starts, surrendering one day and retracting the next, but to abide by our surrender, and go habitually trusting through all the changes we meet, knowing that his love, purpose, and promise are unchangeable. Some little faintings perhaps none are freed from; but I believe a power of trusting the Lord in good measure at all times, and living quietly under the shadow of his wing, is what the promise warrants us to expect, if we seek it by diligent prayer; if not all at once, yet by a gradual increase. May it be your experience and mine!

I am, &c